# MISSING

## INGREDIENTS

*your Bible Study recipe*

Pinchas Shir

ISBN: 9798387178528

# TABLE OF CONTENTS

# INTRODUCTION

Have you ever felt as you read the Bible that it makes no sense? Do you understand the words, but you do not understand the meaning or the point the text is trying to make? The truth is - you are not alone. Every reader of the Bible struggles with finding that ever-elusive meaning from time to time. Every serious student of the Scriptures hits occasional roadblocks. This is exactly why I decided to write this book. Because, after all, we, Bible readers and truth-seekers, are in this boat together.

This book is not intended for someone who is new to the Bible or has never seriously studied it. It is meant for those who took plenty of time but still feel like something is missing. The book is for those who want to go deeper. It is for those who may have lost the zeal to study the Scriptures or feel that their spiritual food tastes ordinary and sort of bland lately.

By the way, the food metaphors I use in the book are intentional. I do see divine words as spiritual food, nutritious and beneficial to every aspect of human lives. Only this food is not a fully prepared meal, but rather raw ingredients. Cooking is all about combining multiple ingredients in a special way and balancing those ingredients. But what a difference the right recipe makes! Enough about food for now. I wrote this book because I have been researching methods of biblical interpretation for years. And in the process, I realized how exciting discovering new angles to reading familiar texts could be. Having overcome many obstacles myself, I have learned how to help others read the Bible better.

Now I can teach others how to dig much deeper into God's timeless words.

I wrote this book because I believe that connecting the dots and understanding God's very words is important for those who take their faith in God seriously. It is exciting and delightful. Many people who read the Bible earnestly yearn to hear from God. Most people of faith know that the wisdom that the Scriptures communicate can be applicable to our everyday lives in profound ways. And we crave such guidance in a way just as children look to their parents for help.

The Spirit of God that lives within us illuminates the meaning of biblical texts for us, and that should never be dismissed. But the Spirit often reveals the parts we need that very day, at that moment, in a highly personal way, not in an objective general sense. What a Bible verse means to me personally and what a verse means, in general, can be two very different things. The people of faith are constantly caught between these two objectives to understand the Bible the way it was originally meant to be understood, the way it was written, and to find ways in which it helps us to live our modern lives today.

I hope you realize that these objectives are connected but not one and the same and create somewhat of a tension. Personal application of Scripture is always in your hands, but my goal as a guide is to lead you to what lies at the foundation – the original meaning. Therefore, in this short book, I share some helpful study methods and techniques that can equip you for the task of understanding the Bible better. Reading and understanding the Bible is simultaneously an art and a skill. And the skill part can always be developed.

In my book title, I mention "Missing Ingredients" because I believe there are several things that are commonly missing in a typical Bible study process. Each time these Bible study ingredients can be added into the process, they produce better results. They give dimensions to the ancient words, they clarify, and they supply nuances. They take us further into the possibilities of what God intended for us to hear and understand and why he chose to speak in that way. Sometimes even those of us who had formal training in studying the Bible miss these important ingredients. So just as in cooking, when the recipe lacks something, the dish may be edible but not as tasty as it could have been if those ingredients were used!

I also know that some Bible readers out there have never tasted the Bible with these ingredients. They don't know what they are missing. They do not realize that there is so much flavor out there. But the moment they try, they will not want to ever go back. So, allow me to explain what I think is missing in many Bible studies. Read on...

Pinchas Shir

Nissan 5, 5783    ה' ניסן תשפ"ג

# WHAT IS MISSING?

In this book, I deliberately compare studying the Bible with cooking an elaborate meal. Why? Because the Bible offers substance, nutrients, and nourishment for the soul that can be easily compared with diverse flavors and benefits of a satisfyingly delicious meal. And making a dish usually includes using a number of ingredients combined and prepared in specific ways and in a certain sequence. The Bible uses human language, and this language is not random. I personally enjoy cooking. It's a hobby both my wife and I share in common. And even more, I love sharing the food I cook with friends who appreciate the process. I often enjoy sharing what went into a meal as I share it with people. For many knowing such things only enhances the dining experience.

In our Bible reading and in cooking, some level of skill is always involved. You must have some understanding of the basics of the process and be skilled enough not to mess up. The process of cooking is not haphazard or random but deliberate and intentional. Both in our Bible study and in at the stove, there are the right kitchen tools, utensils, pots, and pans that we use to do the job. Sorry if I get carried away with the cooking analogies, but I truly feel that they are effective and easy ways to explain our experience with God's words. So, imagine for a moment that studying the Bible is like following a recipe.

We often inherit recipes from family members and friends. Sometimes we improve those recipes and even invent new ones based on some special preferences we have. It's very similar when it comes to reading and studying the Bible.

You may be surprised, but at some point, someone modeled how one should study the Bible for us, showed us how it can be done shared their methodology of the study. Someone taught us how to derive meaning from those ancient texts. Maybe even how to arrive at the application of the truths we glean. Thus, you developed a taste, an expectation of what the final results of studying the Bible should look like. Whether the study method was good or bad, most of us don't even remember when and how we learned how to read and make sense of the Bible. It just happened organically at some point in time, and now we are used to it. And our expectations are based on our past experiences.

Very few people receive formal and intentional training in Bible study methods. If you have, then then you know that the process is very orderly, often with multiple steps, and you certainly grasp my kitchen analogies. But even if what I am describing is not clear. No worries, I will show you what I mean.

What I am suggesting is very simple. People cook the way they know how to cook. They study the Bible with whatever level of skills they possess and with methods they have picked up along the way. I am often faced with this reality when I discuss the Bible with people. I realize that my follow Bible readers follow different recipes for cooking the same dish. They study their Bible differently, the way they learned it. Sometimes the goals are different, and sometimes, the process. But I have spent a lot of time analyzing how and why different people can read the same set of Bible verses and walk away with radically different understandings. Over the years of teaching and discussing the Bible with people from all walks of life, I realized that there are some important ingredients that make my study what it is. Then to my amazement, I discovered that many people do not use these very ingredients at all. This is what this book is about.

So, what are these "missing ingredients" in the study of biblical texts? I will name the three big ones... Language, History, and Cultural Context.

Please don't misunderstand me. I am not saying that you or countless other Bible readers are not able to read the Bible and figure out what it says without these key ingredients. You can. And you may have been doing so quite successfully for many years. What I am saying is - you can do it better with these ingredients in hand! If you choose to intentionally focus on these three key areas in the process of examining the Bible, your study will always produce deeper and richer insights. The Bible verses you think you know, the familiar words will come alive in a completely new way by adding these three ingredients to the mix.

The Bible is a divine message uttered through human words. We are bound to struggle with grasping heavenly wisdom because we are earthly, so focused on our existence and our problems, our perspective on life. The very language of the Bible is foreign to most of us. The

Bible was written in ancient languages that most people do not know or even speak today. So it takes special expertise to peek into the original text.

The ideas the Bible expresses are wrapped up in ancient near eastern cultural contexts. Every message has a proper setting that was meant to be shared and understood by the insiders, those who were involved with that message. Most modern people are not familiar with the ancient world from which God's words call out to them. Make no mistake, when we read the Bible, we enter a world that is significantly unlike our own, sometimes shocking and at other times confusing. No wonder we struggle to connect the dots!

I have a saying about the Bible that I am very fond of - "The text matters, but the context changes everything!" Because the Bible is a text, it is a second-hand experience for us. We are removed from reality, and the geography, the smell, the taste, the weather, the smiles, the frowns, and the actual being there context of the text can be elusive. Yet once we figure some of it out, it truly transforms our understanding of the text. I am going to illustrate this over and over in this book.

For many curious Bible readers, the journey begins with simple discoveries. Take the name, Jesus, for example. When Joseph was upset about the pregnancy of his betrothed, he was visited by an angel who explained, "She will bear a son, and you are to name him Jesus, for he will save his people from their sins." (Mat 1:21 NRSV). He will save people from their sins. That makes sense. Yet it seems that the angel should have said something like, "you are to name him 'Savior' because 'he will save' his people from their sins." But instead, he said, "Jesus" (Ἰησοῦς, *Iesus*), and that is not even close to the word "Savior" (σωτήρ, *soter*) in Greek. The angel was not speaking Greek, and that is why the sentence makes no sense once in Greek or in the English translation of Greek. The puzzle is very easily resolved if you realize that behind the Greek *Iesus* is a Hebrew name Yeshua (יֵשׁוּעַ). And Hebrew name Yeshua actually does come from *yeshuah* (יְשׁוּעָה), the word for "salvation" or "rescue." It's a shortened version of the biblical name Joshua, or *Yehoshua* (יְהוֹשֻׁעַ), which was rendered into the old Greek as *Iesus* (Ἰησοῦς). The logic of the words spoken by the angel makes sense only in Hebrew or Aramaic because the Greek "Jesus" (Ἰησοῦς, *Iesus*) has no traceable connection to the idea of "salvation." The Hebrew name Yeshua, the same as *yeshuah* (יְשׁוּעָה), "salvation" is derived from the verb (יָשַׁע, *yasha*) to "rescue." So order not to lose sight of this meaning will use the name Jesus and Yeshua interchangeably throughout this book.

I invite you to take a journey with me through this book as I explain these three key ingredients and demonstrate what happens when you do not use them and what happens when you do. I will use vivid examples of Bible passages you probably know, but I will add the missing ingredients to the process, and you will see how that recipe will come out. Ready to taste something different?

# THE FIRST MISSING INGREDIENT

It is not a secret that most Bible readers have little or no training in ancient Hebrew and Greek. The entire Hebrew Bible (which Christians call the Old Testament) was written in ancient Hebrew, a language completely unlike English. Well, there is a bit of Aramaic there, but most of it is in Hebrew. The New Testament was written in ancient Greek, which also differs considerably from English. The flow of thought and grammar in these languages is very different from the way we most think today. Even those who speak modern Hebrew and modern Greek, are lost and disoriented once they crack the original texts of the Bible.

Throughout history, Bible translators had to work very hard to make sure those ancient texts make sense to modern English speakers. And we have many excellent English translations that strive to relate the original text as faithfully as they can. Yet translation is always interpretive. Some more, some less but in the end, the translators decide how to best present what they read and understand. That is why we have so many different translations into English.

Most people read the Bible in their own native language, in translation, and while that is wonderful, it can also be problematic. With the ease and comfort of reading biblical texts in our native language, we forget that the world of the Bible is vastly different from our own. We inadvertently begin to imagine and interpret the Bible in light of our modern life.

Ancient Israelites become just like us. That is not entirely bad if we are seeking to connect God's wisdom to our personal lives, but not very helpful at the stage of initial perception and interpretation. Application is usually the last stage of Scripture interpretation. And my advice, keep it that way. Our contemporary thinking, our own linguistic concepts, and cultural connotations lead us away from the ancient meaning of the text and into something we shaped for ourselves, something thoroughly contemporary. We can take wrong interpretive turns and arrive somewhere far from what was originally intended. Would that be us twisting God's words? Even if unintentionally, probably yes.

Consider how simple words we use can change meaning just over the lives of one generation. In antiquity, a "tablet" used to mean "a flat surface object," often wood, coated with wax, designed for writing or carving. Another meaning of "tablet" was "a dose of medicine shaped into a flat and easy-to-swallow shape," most commonly called "a pill" today. Not so long ago, we used the word "tablet" to designate "multiple sheets of paper bound together," a flat notepad on which one could draw or take notes. And the most contemporary meaning of "tablet" today is a portable computing device with a powerful microprocessor, which is used for entertainment, work, videography, person-to-person communication, commerce, and a myriad of other tasks. This is just one simple word and its familiar recent uses. This transformation of the word spans one lifetime. Now imagine thousands of years pass and how much the meaning of a single world can be transformed. Plus, we can think of radically different things when hearing the same exact word, even in English, all depending on the context and on the meaning with which we are most familiar.

Our mind intuitively takes the meaning of words we know best and the ones we perceive to be appropriate and applies it to what we perceive in a world we experience. We do this automatically, intuitively, and often under the influence of the greater context and awareness. A "game" can refer to a board game, to hide-and-seek activity in the backyard, or to a computer game. At the same time, it can be referring to a sports tournament or to an Olympic event. But then we can use it idiomatically to mean "a strategy" or "a trick" or a "shrewd skill in life" of business and even a profession. And what about prey captured during the hunt? We call that "game" as well. When people taste the meat of wild animals, they speak of it tasting "gamy." Confusing? Just imagine learning English as your secondary language and trying to make sense of it all as I once did. I think you see my point.

Words have very divergent meanings, and some of the meanings are way more obscure than others. Some are more archaic, and others have been invented in the last few years. This is English, but Greek and Hebrew do that too. The Bible is pretty old, and thus we struggle to connect the dots because even if we have a good dictionary, we forget that words can change meaning over time. It's a simple omission.

Reading the Bible in translation is a wonderful experience and a great blessing, but every translation is an interpretation of those who are picking the right words in the target language. Translations are subjective by virtue of being translations. Human translators are not perfect, and frankly, if you speak more than one language, you probably know that some words simply do not translate from one language to another because they have no exact equivalents. We can get close, but we rarely have an exact equivalent when it comes to translations. Many years ago, I actually ran a translating and interpreting business for a while. I had to learn how to interpret quickly in various settings and how to translate texts of very diverse topics. My vocabulary was very broad, but every time it was I who decided which word would represent the term I was to translate the best.

Take the Hebrew word עוֹלָם (olam), for example. Its is a very common word in Hebrew. But it is notoriously hard to translate accurately into English. As a noun, it is often translated as "world" as in a popular phrase "the world to come" *olam haba*. Another alternative is "age" in a temporal sense, an "era," an "epoch." But that is not all. It is also common to translate this term as "everlasting" and "forever", sometimes even as "eternity."

When the Hebrew Bible speaks of something lasting for a long time, for an age, or in perpetuity, is uses this unique word עוֹלָם (olam). So does it mean forever, as in something that never ends, or does it mean for a certain age, i.e., a timespan, people ask? The truth is – both. The temporal idea the word expresses is not determined; it can be unlimited or with an end in sight depending completely on the context. Now try to find an appropriate word in English that would express all these ideas simultaneously. Good luck. It does not exist.

And picking any one of the above-used alternatives would never be a true and fully fair translation. It would be a situational suggestion that would lead the reader in one or another direction, limiting the perception to an option you, as a translator, propose but not orient the reader to see all other aspects of the original term simultaneously. The word עוֹלָם (olam) simply does not have an equivalent that would do it justice. So we settle for what is best in our judgment, realizing that the full meaning of עוֹלָם (olam) cannot be fully captured by any single English word. Such is the frequent limitation of translating from any human language to another. Some languages may be close, especially if they are related. But the less languages are alike, the more confusing such translations can be. Hebrew is a Semitic language, and perhaps a cognate language will have a closer and better translation of עוֹלָם (olam), but English does not.

Naturally, because the majority of Bible readers are not able to dig deep into the original text of the Bible, they only see the words the translators chose for them and then interpret those choices (offered to them) through the lens of their personal understanding. This is why Bible readers periodically make gross errors in judgment, often leaning on the English text too much and not looking any further. Trusting those who know languages better than you do is reasonable, but being able to verify what they are saying gives us the assurance that we are trusting the right experts and they did their job superbly. So nothing can truly replace language training and expertise.

An appropriate example comes to mind. One semester I was asked to teach a course on campus for my colleague. Fortunately, I was asked well in advance, so I had time to prepare. But I did not have time to re-work the syllabus, so I ended up using the books he planned to use for his lectures. One of the books was called "Eternity in Their Hearts" by Don Richardson. It was an excellent book, I thought, quite inspirational and written by a missionary who understood the nuances of language and translation. The author had a somewhat warped view of Jews, but I am accustomed to that in Christian publications, so I used the book in my lectures anyway.

Delving deeper into the book, I encountered Don Richardson's explanation of Jesus overturning the tables in the Temple court of the gentiles. Suddenly, I stumbled across one of those gross misunderstandings based solely on the use of language. Though my students did not notice, I could hardly believe it as I read and re-read his explanations. The author wrote:

> "It was the only part of the Temple that Gentile tourists or even devout Gentile "God-fearers" were allowed to enter. It was God's purpose that Gentiles entering that Sacred precinct **would hear Jews praying for them**, and would know unmistakably that the God of the Jews was truly the God of the whole

Earth and God who desired to bless all peoples."

Then creatively imaging the reasoning of the Temple authorities, Richardson continued:

> "It occurred to them that the area called the Court of the Gentiles was not really being put too much use. After all, **who really prays for Gentiles anymore**? And if anyone **wants to pray for Gentiles** he could do it anywhere. Was it really practical to tie up an entire area of high-potential real estate for a pursuit as unpopular as **praying for Gentiles**? "Rezone the Court of the Gentiles for commercial use!" thus became a popular campaign issue."

So what's the problem? For those who know, the "court of the gentiles was the largest part of Herod's Jerusalem Temple complex, where any outsiders (non-Jews) were allowed to enter and participate in Israel's worship these words sound strange. Richardson was convinced that the plaza (called the court of the nations/gentiles) was designed "for Jews to pray for gentiles." He repeats this belief several times in the quotes above. But when King Solomon was praying at the time of the Temple dedication, he famously proclaimed that the prayers of foreigners will also be heard if they join Israel and pray "towards the holy place." The court of the nations was designed to accommodate the worship of everyone, even complete outsiders to the covenant.

41 "Likewise, **when a foreigner, who is not of your people Israel**, comes from a far country for your name's sake 42 (for they shall hear of your great name and your mighty hand, and of your outstretched arm), **when he comes and prays toward this house** (וְהִתְפַּלֵּל אֶל־הַבַּיִת הַזֶּה, *vehitpalel el habait hazeh)*, 43 hear in heaven your dwelling place and do according to all for which the foreigner calls to you, in order that all the peoples of the earth may know your name and fear you, as do your people Israel, and that they may know that this house that I have built is called by your name. (1 Kings 8:41-43 NASB)

So were the foreigners supposed to be praying themselves in the Temple? Or were Jews supposed to be praying for them? Richardson was quite emphatic that Jews were supposed to be praying for gentiles in the court of the gentiles and that they failed at this task miserably. That is why Richardson explained Jesus was so upset when he saw the commerce in that area reserved for such prayers.

So I had to ask myself, how did it happen that Don Richardson misunderstood the very purpose of the court of the gentiles so profoundly? My best guess is he trusted whichever English translation he was reading and simply made a wrong conclusion based on his errant understanding of the text.

The misunderstood verse is probably Isaiah 56:7, which says, "my house will be called a house of prayer for all nations" (NIV, NKJV, NLT) or "a house of prayer for all peoples" (KJV, ESV, NASB). The problem is the English preposition "for." It creates a certain ambiguity. It can lead one to think that the prayer in the house is FOR the nations. Or it can be understood as the nations are to be praying and that house of prayer is FOR them, meaning that it is open FOR them and designated FOR them.

I am fairly confident that the simple misreading of how the preposition should be taken is the cause of this tragic misunderstanding. The original text of Isaiah 56:7 says (כִּי בֵיתִי בֵּית־תְּפִלָּה יִקָּרֵא לְכָל־הָעַמִּים, *ki beiti beit tefilah yikrah lekol haamim)* and I would translate the sentence this way - "for my house, will be called a house of prayer, for all people." Perhaps you can see how for me and for many Jews throughout history, it is crystal clear that all people (all nations) were meant to be themselves praying in the temple Solomon built and not simply be "prayed for." The problem of such seemingly insignificant misunderstanding does not stop at one verse, however. It forms an errant idea in the book, which the author then uses to explain other verses in the Bible and creates a theological paradigm. That's where it gets a bit more dangerous.

I hope you can see that trusting English translations, no matter how reputable, can lead to misunderstandings. Such instances are not inevitable, but the potential is always there. A simple awareness that English is only a translation, and the original text may need to be consulted, especially when something is not exactly clear, may help avoid such mishaps.

By the way, I firmly believe that most English translations are excellent (and I have my favorites), but I am not under the illusion that they are perfect. Every translation is interpretive and full of human choices. Most people will read the Bible in translation, and though I expect much more from scholars and experts, translations will not lead them astray. Still, recognition of translations' limitations, awareness, and occasional verification of the original text is a powerful tool that changes Bible study for everyone. This awareness of language differences is one of the missing ingredients.

Most of us today cannot imagine what it is like to be illiterate. Unlike the ancient world, we are surrounded by a culture that reads and writes. But imagine you have traveled to a country whose language you do not understand and cannot read it. You rely on people telling you what that sign you see says or what it is written on a product label in the store. It is sour cream or buttermilk? And when someone relates that information to you, they are translating the best they know how, and it is not always perfect or even complete. Though your friends may try their best, things inevitably get lost in translation. Sometimes they don't know the right words; at other times, they can't find the right words because there are no exact equivalents. Now that you can imagine yourself in this scenario, there is where most of us are with the Bible. Translations are super helpful, but they can fall short. And then, on top of less-than-ideal translations, there is our subjective and limited understanding.

Once, I stumbled upon an interesting belief that Jesus was a Nazarite. A Nazarite? Yep, like Samson. The first time I heard this, I had to think hard to figure out how one would come to such a conclusion reading the gospels. And then, I realized that language was to blame for this confusion. The Gospel of Matthew says, "And he came and lived in a city called Nazareth. This was to fulfill what was spoken through the prophets: "He shall be called a Nazarene." (Mat 2:23)

If you do not know this already, the writings of the Apostles, which Christians have entitled "New Testament," are actually Jewish literary works. Though the authors wrote in Greek, there is always some Hebrew lurking behind their words. The writers whose works became known as the New Testament wrote in Koine Judeo-Greek (colloquial Greek of Jews), and sometimes, linguistically speaking, things got messy. Most of the time, the Hebrew that stands behind the Greek is hard to see, especially after the text was translated into English. So if you want to see the source of confusion, you will have to go beyond English and Greek in this case.

Nazarene is not the same as Nazarite. There are very different words, but English does not help us to see this. You guessed it, Hebrew shows this very clearly! The oldest manuscripts of Matthew 2:23 are in Greek, and the two terms *Nazareth* and *Nazarene* seem to be connected. Indeed, in Greek, both terms Ναζαρέτ (*natzaret*) and Ναζωραῖος *(nazoraios)* look really similar! But what is crucial to understand is that these are actually not Greek words but Hebrew. Both words derive from the original Hebrew root נֵצֶר *(netzer)*, which means "branch," "shoot," or "sprout." That is presumably the meaning for the town of Nazareth Ναζαρέτ / נָצְרַת *(natzaret)* in Hebrew, a "place of the shoot" or "place of the sprout."

So is the word Nazarene connected to the word Nazarite? Well, not in Hebrew. In Hebrew, the word "Nazarite" is נָזִיר *(nazir)*. It always describes someone "consecrated" or "devoted" to God. It's a fairly unique term. Notice that it is spelled with the letter Zayn (the second letter from the right). But please notice that the second letter in נֵצֶר *(netzer)* is not *Zayin* but *Tzadeh* (second letter from the right). The two different Hebrew letters even sound similar - ז (z) and צ (tz), but they are not the same letters. These two Hebrew letters may even be phonetically represented by the same letters in Greek and in English, but they are, in fact, entirely distinct letters.

If I lost you, I apologize, but what I am trying to show is that נָצְרַת *(natzaret)*, the town of Nazareth, and Nazarite - נָזִיר *(nazir)* are not related to each other in the original language from which they emerge. They may sound as if they were related, but their native Hebrew spellings differ. Greek spellings are not crucial in this case because these are Hebrew words spelled using Greek letters. Looking at the Greek (Ναζαρέτ and Ναζωραῖος), one may think that the words are related, but they are not. Their meanings are not related to each other. It's like saying that a "reed" is similar to "red" and thus, all reeds are red. The reason this confusion exists is an inaccurate perception due to seeming similarity.

By the way, if you are curious, Nazareth נְצֶרֶת *(natzaret)* in Hebrew implies that it is a town of a "branch," a "shoot," or a "sprout." It most likely refers to the Messiah as he is described by the prophets (Is 11:1) or maybe to the people of Israel themselves (Is. 60:21). And a Nazarene in Hebrew is נוֹצְרִי *(notzri)*. Coincidently the word for "Christians" in modern Hebrew is נוֹצְרִיים *(notzriim)* – those who follow a Nazarene.

So, no, Jesus was not a Nazarite. When Yeshua, the son of Yosef, was called a Nazarene, he was associated with the geographic location from which he came, namely the town of Galilee. And colloquially speaking, that was not even a positive or flattering reference. Many inhabitants of Judea looked down on rural Galilean Jews and thought of them as uncultured, uneducated farmers, simpletons who spoke with a strange provincial accent. So what difference does it make if someone thinks that Jesus was a Nazarite? *Nazirut* is not something bad. True, but Jesus clearly did not live the life of a Nazarite. To portray him as a Nazarite is to twist his image into something he never was or claimed to be and suggest a way of living he did not embrace.

No matter what part of the Bible we read, it can be puzzling. We can get side-tracked and miss beautiful truths because our misunderstanding of language leads us astray. In the Gospel of John, for example, Jesus says, "No one has ascended into heaven except he who descended from heaven, the Son of Man" (John 3:13). If you are a Bible student, you know that this seems to contradict biblical accounts of certain people entering the heavenly realm.

Elijah was whisked from our world into heaven. Jewish tradition holds that God snatched Enoch in a similar manner. Did Yeshua forget these instances? No, the contradiction is only in our minds or, more precisely, in the meaning that we take away from the words he spoke. A closer look that the original terms used in the Bible will clarify what Messiah claimed and did not claim. This is where being able to look into the Greek text is invaluable.[1]

Elijah did not taste death but was lifted into heaven. The Greek text of the Septuagint states, "Behold, a chariot of fire and horses of fire [appeared]... and Elijah "was taken up" (ἀνελήμφθη; *anelemphthe*) as in a whirlwind into heaven" (2 Kings 2:11 LXX). In this case, God sent a divine chariot to whisk Elijah from the earth. He traveled as a passive passenger. Likewise, Enoch lived a life walking with God, and then Septuagint says, "was not found, because the Almighty "transferred him" (μετέθηκεν αὐτὸν; *metetheken auton*)" (Gen 5:24 LXX).

So, in John, Jesus says of himself that "no one has "ascended" (ἀναβέβηκεν; *anabebeken*) into heaven except he who descended from heaven, the Son of Man" (John 3:13). And he is being very precise. The word for "ascend" (ἀναβαίνω) literally means to "walk up." Yeshua is the only one who actually "walked up" to

---

1 For this cogent explanation, I am indebted to my colleague Dr. Schaser.

heaven on his own accord. Enoch and Elijah were taken to heaven as passive participants. But the Son of Man walked up there because he could. Unlike other holy men, Yeshua could come down and go up on his own. Therefore, the words he uttered are meant to set him apart from others who made a similar journey. He is the first in human history who can decide to go up, and just do it. Being able to look at this in the original language removes the ambiguity.

The inability to switch between ancient Greek and Hebrew freely can be an obstacle and can create confusion for the casual reader, especially if we consider the original audience shifted between several languages. Ancient Jews lived in a multilingual environment and often navigated multiple languages simultaneously. In an ideal world, we would be able to switch with them.

While English translations can inadvertently create plenty of confusion, trust me, most Bible translations never wish to mislead anyone intentionally. There is no grand conspiracy to keep the truth from anyone. Most modern English Bible translations are quite good, in fact, but the nuances of the text are all buried in the original language. And while the core of the message is usually not hard to ascertain, those nuances do not carry over into other languages so easily. Things do get lost in translation, and most often, completely unintentionally.

::::::: I hope you are enjoying the book! If you do, would you help others to discover it? It will take only 5 minutes of your time. Pull up the title of this book inside Amazon, tap "write a customer review," and leave a few meaningful remarks. You

Sometimes translations can inadvertently create contradictions that could be tricky to resolve. Let me share another vivid example. Once, I received a curious question from a man who was struggling to read through the book of Hebrews in the New Testament. His question had to do with the Temple layout and with the Tabernacle arrangement, which was originally described in the book of Exodus.

The problem that he discovered was this. In Exodus, the מִזְבַּח הַקְּטֹרֶת *(mizbeach haketoret)* "the altar of incense" was stationed in the Holy Place. The Torah is very clear about this. In Hebrews 9:4, however, the text said that the incense was in the Holy of Holies. If you studied the Tabernacle layout, you know that "Holy Place" and "Holy of Holies" are not the same. So how can this be? This is what the book of Hebrews says:

> "Behind the second curtain was a tent called the Holy of Holies. In it stood the **golden altar of incense** and the ark of the covenant overlaid on all sides with gold, in which there were a golden urn holding the manna, and Aaron's rod that budded, and the tablets of the covenant" (Hebrews 9:3-4 NRSV).

The Holy Place and Holy of Holies were two separate rooms sectioned off by a curtain in the wilderness

27

Tabernacle. According to Flavius Josephus, Herod's Temple had not only a curtain but also large doors separating the sections. The Holy of Holies was visited only once a year and was supposed to contain only the Ark of the Covenant with its contents. The מִזְבַּח הַקְּטֹרֶת *(mizbeach haketoret)* – the altar of incense" was supposed to be on the other side of the separation in the Holy Place and not in the Holy of Holies as the text of Hebrews 9:3-4 suggests. To get a closer look at the original, I opened a Greek-English Interlinear New Testament, and everything seemed in order. So then I decided to investigate what the book of Exodus says:

> "He put the **golden altar** in the tent of meeting before the curtain and offered fragrant incense on it; as the Lord had commanded Moses" (Exodus 40:26-27 NRSV)

Was the writer of Hebrews not familiar with this arrangement? Did he not know the Torah? Did he make a mistake concerning the arrangement of holy articles in the Tabernacle? There certainly appears to be a discrepancy of some sort between these two texts.

The answer to this lies right in the text. Only not in English. The book of Hebrews was written in Greek in the first century CE, and the Torah was written in Hebrew and naturally much, much earlier. But also, a couple of centuries before the Common Era, Torah was already translated into Greek, probably in Alexandria, Egypt. The translation is called Septuagint today (abbreviated as LXX), and many Greek-speaking Jews utilized this translation for their study and worship in Hellenistic times. So I opened a Greek-English Septuagint to investigate further.

In the Greek translation of Exodus 40:1 the "altar of incense" was rendered as θυσιαστήριον θυμιάματος *(thusiasterion thmiamatos)*. It is a straightforward translation from Hebrew where θυσιαστήριον *(thusiasterion)* means "the altar." In Greek θυσία *(thusia)* is "an offering," and θυμιάματος *(thumiamatos)* is the word for "incense." So, this is a good and literal translation of Hebrew into Greek.

When one takes a closer look at Hebrews 9:4 in Greek, one would expect to find the word θυσιαστήριον *(thusiasterion)* in the text, just like in the Septuagint translation of Exodus. That is the word that means "altar," and that would be a proper equivalent in the Koine Greek to render the original term מִזְבֵּחַ *(mizbeach)* found in the Torah. But instead, in the Hebrews passage, we will find the word θυμιατήριον *(thumiaterion),* which does not mean "an altar." The words do look a little bit alike to an untrained eye, but θυσία *(thusia)* is an "offering," and θυμίαμα *(thumiama)* is an "incense," and these are not the same! I used Thayer's Greek-English Lexicon to compare the meanings.

Apologies if I lost you again… I will get to the point. This Greek word θυμιατήριον *(thumiaterion)* is a technical description of "something that holds incense," but not necessarily "the altar of the incense" itself. It could be logically assumed that the altar is that which holds the incense. But it is also possible that something else does. It should be clarified that the Greek word θυσιαστήριον *(thusiasterion)* – "altar" does not appear in the Greek text of Hebrews 9:3-4 at all. The English word "altar" was supplied by the translators for clarity. I could see that by examining the text in the Greek-English Interlinear New Testament. In the same manner, the verb "stood" is also not in the original text. In its place is the verb "to have." In trying to be helpful, the translators supplied the language they felt that makes more sense to the English-speaking audience. If you have not connected the dots yet, here is the solution to the seeming contradiction. How can incense be present in the Holy of Holies without the altar? Ezekiel 8:11 and its Greek wording might be very helpful in resolving this.

"Before them stood seventy of the elders of the house of Israel, with Jaazaniah son of Shaphan standing among them. Each had his **censer** in his hand, **and the fragrant cloud of incense was ascending**" (Ezekiel 8:11 NRSV).

The word θυμιατήριον *(thuimaterion)* appears in the second part of verse 11, and there it is translated as "a censer." In Hebrew "censer" is מִקְטֶרֶת *(mikteret)*. It is a vessel that holds incense. It is a portable item and is hard to confuse with the altar, which is usually stationary. In Ezekiel's text, each man held this item in one's hand.

In Hebrews 9, the text clearly describes the priestly service in the Holy of Holies. It is not a secret that according to Lev. 16:13, the High Priest was instructed to take the incense with him into the Most Holy place in order that the smoke would obscure the view of the Ark, the place of God's very presence. This was done by taking with him a portable device, yes, a censer full of incense. Such a keen understanding of the priestly ritual would explain why the writer of Hebrews shows the presence of a censer in the Holy of Holies in Hebrews 9:4.

This may have been a drawn-out explanation, but I wanted to show you the process of how a contradiction in the English text can be resolved through the investigation of the original language. The Greek text of Hebrews 9:3-4 reveals that behind the curtain in the Holy of Holies was a censer and not an altar of incense. A mistranslation caused a discrepancy in where things were positioned. The author of Hebrews was not mistaken after all, and an unfortunate translation is really to blame for the confusion.

Answers to many confusing questions in the Bible often can be found by examining the original texts in their original languages, by looking at precise words used, and by studying how these words were used elsewhere in ancient texts and what they meant. That is all I did in this scenario to unravel what seemed like a contradiction.

Sometimes seemingly insignificant nuances can make a huge difference. Being able to perceive that someone is using playful, poetic, or idiomatic language, humor, irony, technical language, some form of wordplay, or inflammatory words is key to understanding the context.

Original terminology can turn things around completely. Insights that come from understanding the original languages can transform the meaning of what is being said. **Thus, the ability to examine biblical texts in original languages is the missing ingredient number one.**

But what if I tell you that sometimes translations do not lose but find things that are not even there, to begin with? Would you believe me? An old Christian hymn evokes God's help to never to forget the suffering of Jesus – "King of my life, I crown Thee now, Thine shall the glory be; lest I forget Thy thorn-crowned brow, lead me to Calvary… Lest I forget Thy love for me, lead me to Calvary." These are heartfelt and meaningful words of praise. You can almost feel the emotion of the person who composed these words. But you might be shocked… There was no such place as Calvary in ancient Jerusalem.

Search all over the New Testament, and you will not find it. You will not find it in any of the gospel passages describing how Jesus was executed. Let me clarify. You may find it in some English translations but not in the Greek text. Mark, Matthew, and John all mention Golgotha – a word which, according to them, translates as "the place of the skull." Luke also mentions the "skull place" but does not mention the original Semitic name associated with that spot.

Three gospels mention that Golgotha is a Hebrew word, though no one is certain if it was truly Hebrew, Aramaic, or some mixture of the two. In Aramaic גָּלְגָּלְתָּא

*(gulgulita)* could mean a skull or a head. According to the Dictionary of the Targumim (Jastrow), it means "a round stone" or "a ball." The association with the round-shaped skull makes sense. But that is not exactly the same as Γολγοθά *(golgotha)* - the original word preserved in the Greek manuscripts. So we are actually not sure about the original term, and we are left with the translations supplied to us by the gospel authors themselves.

Indeed, Golgotha was a real place situated somewhere outside the walls of first-century Jerusalem, not far from the garden with tombs of wealthy people. But the name *Calvary* comes from the Latin word *calvaria,* which translates as "skull." The word Calvary was not in use in Jesus's day in the gospel stories. Jesus' followers did not call the place where he died Calvary. Only after Jerome created the Latin Vulgate translation of the Bible (late 4th century), the word came into gradual Christian use.

So here is the mystery – *Calvary* is not a biblical word, but rather a post-biblical one. Today people sing songs about Calvary, not even realizing they are using a Latin word from the Catholic Vulgate translation of the original Aramaic. Calvary is not really a biblical word since the first-century inhabitants of Jerusalem and the gospel writers themselves never used it. There is nothing wrong with the term. It's even an accurate translation of the original, only into Latin, not into English. So if you wish to continue to use Latin terminology, then, by all means, continue calling the place of Jesus' death Calvary. But if you want to be biblically and historically accurate, you should call it Γολγοθά *(golgotha)* as the New Testament does.

I realize that this is a banal illustration. No real harm is done here. But language is never superficial. It carries specific meanings, and it conveys vivid images and ideas into our minds. Most people would say, "what's the difference what we call it? Greek, Hebrew, Latin... That does not change anything." I would say it does. Using Latin terms which did not exist in the first century Jerusalem creates a false sense that the setting of those events is not really Jewish. As if it all happened in Rome or somewhere else but not in Judea. Inserting Latin terminology into the gospel narrative is a technique called contextualization, but it moves the story away from its original setting.

The English Bible has already been thoroughly de-Judaized and stripped of its organic Semitic feel over the ages. In the process of translation, people's names and geographical locations have all been changed beyond recognition. Every English speaker knows Moses, but the name Moshe is probably unfamiliar to them. An average reader of the Bible knows James, but not Ya'akov, Jerusalem but not Yerushalaim, Bethany, but not Beit Anya. Many theological ideas and Semitic buzzwords were smoothed out through millennia of redefining the text into other languages to the degree that they are no longer recognizable. Most people do not realize how much things were anglicized in the Bible they read. But you can pick up a Complete Jewish Bible translation and begin reading the New Testament you will quickly see. In this 1980s translation, Dr. David Stern purposefully reversed the practice.

It may seem like a trivial matter, but I would note that this is exactly the reason why people misunderstand so many Biblical passages. The context is missing, so they take the words and ideas out of context, or worse, they supply an alternative context they made up themselves and later wonder why they have a hard time understanding the Bible. I find this at the same time ironic and sad. Unfortunately, there are many other words like Calvary which found their way into the English Bible. Lucifer, for example, in not in the original text of the Bible, and Easter is another misnomer, yet some English Bibles contain them because these words are traditional to the Western church culture. The only way to catch on to such innovations is to look at the Hebrew or Greek text of the Bible.

The Bible was not written in English, and that means the English text is only a translation of God's revelation and not the revelation itself. In fact, throughout history, Jews communicated in multiple languages, Hebrew, Greek, Aramaic, and their ancient texts are a product of this multilingual mix. Of course, Classical Hebrew is the language in which most of the Biblical stories came down to us. But Aramaic, the language spoken by many near-eastern people, was not far behind. Only select portions of the canonical Bible were composed in literary Aramaic, but later the entire Five Books of Moses and many other scrolls were translated into Aramaic and into Greek as well. And these were living languages in which Jews read, recited, and retold those timeless stories.

Sacred texts in Aramaic were used in Synagogue worship and for study for many years. We should never lose sight that many Jews remained in Babylon after the great exile and continued to speak and write in Aramaic. This language was significant in the Jewish world of that day. Today we call the Aramaic translations of the Bible Targums.[2]

With the advance of Greek civilization and the Hellenization of the entire Mediterranean, more and more people began speaking Greek. For Jews, however, the Hebrew and Aramaic did not go really away. Jews simply added the Greek language to the list. Eventually, the utilitarian nature of Greek moved to greater prominence among the Jews. From the second century BCE, many Jews conversed and wrote in Koine Greek, a Judeo-Greek adaptation of the classical language. As a result, many works of Jewish literature of the Hellenistic era were written not in Hebrew but in Greek, a language most common to Jewish people living outside of Israel. The books of the Hebrew Bible began to be translated into Greek as well. And in those days, more than half of Jews lived outside of the borders of their ancestral lands for various reasons. Greek became the language of business, learning, and interaction with the rest of the world, much like English in our day.

---

[2] There is also Peshitta, but it is different from the Targums. The Peshitta is a Syriac (Syrian Aramaic) translation of the Bible done by early Christians between the second and fifth centuries CE.

Take Philo of Alexandria, for example. His writings are all in Greek, and they are quite extensive. But from them, it is very clear that he knows Hebrew quite well as he explains Moses' words and ponders their philosophical applications. And the New Testament was written by Jews in Greek as well. Yet it is apparent that they knew Hebrew and Aramaic as well because they drew a lot of their terminology from both of these languages. Later, Roman dominance brought Latin to the forefront. But at that point, the Jewish community was in a state of decline, decentralized and scattered, so Latin was never embraced by Jews to the degree in which Greek was.

With the destruction of the Temple in 70 CE and leveling of Jerusalem in 136 CE, a lot has changed in the Jewish world. In the east, Aramaic continued to influence Jewish culture quite heavily, so the Hebrew of rabbinic academies was often mixed with Aramaic. Over many years of Jewish dispersion, other languages such as Ladino (Jewish language based on Spanish) and Yiddish (a language influenced by German, Polish, Ukrainian, and Russian) appeared in diverse and distant Jewish communities. But the primary languages which pertained to Biblical studies were always Hebrew, Greek, and Aramaic. These three languages often hold the keys to the understanding of proper terms, names, places, and major ideas. Without interacting with these three languages, deep investigation of many biblical passages becomes almost impossible. So much of the meaning of words depends on the original languages, and sometimes significant things get lost in translation.

I realize that you may feel a bit discouraged at the moment. I just showed you a key missing ingredient in your Bible study but may feel that mastering these ancient biblical languages is out of reach for you. There is no reason to despair! You may not be in a position to spend years studying ancient Greek and Hebrew academically, but you can use wonderful language tools available today, tools specially designed for those who do not have a mastery of biblical languages. Plus, I can offer you some practical guidance on how to move forward.

Unless you are looking for practical advice, please feel free to ignore what comes next. Skipping to the next chapter will not interrupt the flow of this book.

**STEP 1.** A student of the Bible can always begin with a good literal translation (NASB, Young's, NKJV, NRSV) and compare it with less literal ones (NIV, ESV, NET). The differences one notes in English texts alone should be able to give you a clue that the original text may not be very straightforward. This is exactly why different translators have expressed what they read in several different ways.

If you don't already use a good Study Bible, there are so many on the market. Some are better than others. And if I was to recommend only one, I would personally steer you toward this one - Cultural Backgrounds Study Bible. The notes in it are totally worth it!

**STEP 2.** There are many interlinear Bibles in English in print, online, and in software. And I recommend you start using them to study deeper! There are also concordances and dictionaries keyed to English both in print and digital formats. Some are even in the public domain and available online for free. In our high-tech days, the obstacle of not knowing Hebrew and Greek can be minimized with the use of good Bible software. Software may not replace true expertise, but it will give you access to information previously available to very few people.

If I were to recommend one piece of Bible study software, I would tell you about this one - Logos Software. I have been using this particular software for years and find it extremely useful. Besides translations, it puts the Hebrew and Greek texts of the Bible along with dictionaries at my fingertips and saves me a lot of time. Though digital books are a fraction of the price of printed editions, a decent package can still be an investment. But since I use the software all the time for me, it is totally worth it.

STEP 3 Learn how to read biblical languages. How deep you can go into the original text depends on the level to which you want to commit yourself to the study of Hebrew and Greek. Often simply learning basic reading skills in both languages greatly enhances one's ability to examine the original texts. Learning how to read in another language is the first step in seeking deeper understanding. Can you do that? I promise you that it will not take years of study. Plus, an ability to read opens doors to using better and more detailed dictionaries, which expect that the user can read Greek and Hebrew and offer more detailed information.

Just recently, my colleagues and I released a great book for those just starting out- Read Hebrew in 22 Days or Less. If you pick up some vocabulary and take the time to study even some grammar of Hebrew and Greek, you will be even better off. It does not have to be an "all or nothing" approach. I have personally taught eight-year-olds and eighty-year-olds how to read in a new language, and it did not take years.

**STEP 4.** Reach out to experts! There are always experts who know the languages well enough to be able to consult and answer questions about the text. Knowing the basics of Greek and Hebrew helps a lot when such answers are given. My students often ask me questions about various text translations, and most of the time, I can point them in the right direction. They learn, grow and move to the next steps, often offering their help to others.

Whatever level you will resolve to achieve in accessing the original text, adding this missing ingredient of language to your Bible study will produce better results each time. Even simple awareness of these issues will steer you in the right direction.

# THE SECOND MISSING INGREDIENT

Many Bible readers know little about the history behind the text they are studying. What just happened as these particular words were spoken? Who are the people involved in the story you are reading? What role do they play in the world of that day? Are they important, powerful or an oppressed subgroup without a voice? What is the audience the writer is aiming at? What did the writers and their listeners experience at the moment of these verses being written? What was happening in the city, town, or village where they resided? Is geographic location at all important to the context? There are many questions that we can ask of the text, and we don't always have all answers. But even surface awareness of such issues can be of great help when it comes to an understanding what we read better.

History can seem quite boring to people; dates, sequences of events, names of influential people, achievements of those in charge, details, details, details and etc... Our knowledge of ancient history is limited. There is so much to know about the ancient world, and we have many knowledge gaps. We are not sure about many dates, and sometimes ancient historians are more like storytellers and playwrights. But we do have some good ideas about the past in general, and that is a good place to start. While many details may be unknown, we do know the big picture most of the time, and this picture shares the values of the ancient world with us.

What is important to appreciate is that the historical moment in which we live today right now frames the world we experience in so many multi-faceted ways. It defines the opinions and ideas we express and even gives reasons as to why we say what we say and how we mean what we say. In a way, knowing the historical reality in which we live may be a key to understanding what we think and say.

Imagine me speaking on racial injustice on the day Barak Obama became the President of the United States of America - that's one particular historical setting. But what if I speak the same exact words about racial injustice in America when Black Lives Matter crowds demonstrate in the streets of major US cities burning down police cars? My words have not changed, but that is an entirely different historical setting. In each scenario, the words I speak will be received and be understood in the context of the historical setting in which they were expressed. If you were to listen to my racial injustice speech one hundred years later or one hundred years earlier, my words might not make any sense! They will not ring the same without the knowledge of the proper context and occasion to which they were tied. If you do not catch on to my speech's historical setting, the meaning and intent of my speech will most likely be misconstrued.

Every communication that occurs usually occurs for a reason, and it occurs in some specific context. The message cannot be carelessly divorced from that native context. If it is divorced from the original setting, its meaning will not be sustained faithfully. And any communication without the awareness to its context can lose its true meaning and can be easily misunderstood and twisted to mean something it was never intended to communicate. Such is the nature of human communication.

The Bible may offer us timeless words, but those words came to us through a concrete setting, in a specific language, attached to a particular time and place. Knowing that setting when those words were spoken gives us a point of reference and can help us see deeper into the meanings of those words. **Therefore, I believe that knowledge of historical setting is the missing ingredient number two.** If we ignore the moment and the occasion in which the biblical message we read was born and delivered, were are missing quite a bit.

It's an easy omission to make. And the task of knowing some historical background can be a true challenge. Nevertheless, if we want a better understanding, that is what it will take. Being unaware of historical realities puts us in a position to miss out on what is really going on in those timeless stories in the Bible.

Consider this scenario. In the gospel passion narratives, after the last supper, Jesus ascends to the Mount of Olives with his disciples. They are in the garden at nighttime. Amidst the olive trees, Jesus prays to God about what is to come. It is a moment of agony, and Jesus is visibly uneasy. He has no doubts of the importance of the moment, but in his humanity, he struggles with what is approaching. He prays, "remove this cup from me" (Mark 14:29, Luke 22:42) In

Matthew's story, he says, "my Father, if it is possible, let this cup pass from me" (Mat. 26:39).

What cup? Is this just a quaint phrase, or is there a deeper context behind it? Numerous Christian commentaries refer to this cup as the "cup of God's wrath," citing Psalm 11:6 and Isaiah 51:17 as background passages to his words. Jesus will take sin upon himself and will have to carry its weight. The same ideas appear in another passage where Jesus asks his disciples, "Are you able to drink the cup that I drink or to be baptized with the baptism with which I am baptized?" (Mark 10:38).

In this context, the cup, of course, is not a literal cup but an idiom that stands for what Jesus must endure, his future fate. An insightful reader can catch on to this without too much effort. Yeshua is speaking about his death, not some cup. Jesus predicted his sufferings and tried to explain to his disciples a number of times what would occur. But there is a rich cultural context and many ancient customs that stand behind Jesus' seemingly idiomatic language. His language is not generic but very specific. His words are very time-sensitive and are tied to the historical moment when they were spoken.

To see it clearly, you must consider the setting of the feast of Passover as the timing of his comments. The cup that Jesus wished would pass may refer to a very particular cup dramatized during the formal Passover meal that many Jews celebrated back then. Most Bible readers realize that Jesus was celebrating Passover just hours before, but since they are more familiar with Easter celebrations in their church and don't know enough about Jewish Passover rituals the contextual meaning of Yeshua's Passover-themed prayer usually goes unnoticed.

You should know that there are disagreements among scholars about whether Jesus really celebrated Passover with his disciples. Some claim that the last supper was just a meal before Passover, and others insist on the literal Passover feast context. Regardless, Jesus kept repeating the phrase "this cup," and perhaps the first-century readers saw something more in this phrase because they were familiar with such phraseology. In fact, I am convinced they were. Though Jesus's modern interpreters are scarcely aware of how Passover was celebrated during the first century, there are some great historical sources that may share relevant cultural details. One place I often look is Mishna.

In Mishna,[3] in Pesahim 10, the Passover celebrants drink four cups of wine in remembrance of the four stages of God's deliverance from Egypt. The four cups and the symbolism behind them are inspired by the four divine promises found in Ex 6:6-7. The evening meal is a remembrance and reenactment of the Passover journey step by step. The evidence from Jewish literature suggests that many of the Passover rituals explained in Mishna and both Talmuds[4] existed long before the temple was destroyed and were most likely present in

---

[3] An early rabbinic text from the second century CE.
[4] There are two versions of the Talmud. Each consists of the base text of Mishna, supplied by a commentary. The Jerusalem Talmud was compiled by the rabbis in the land of Israel, and Babylonian Talmud was compiled by the rabbis in Babylonia.

the days of Jesus. Some of them can even be traced through the gospel's accounts. And I think this is exactly the case here with the cup. The tradition of four cups at Passover dinner is a significant cultural context to consider.

For example, in Mishna, the third and the fourth cup of Passover are connected with the singing of הַלֵּל (*hallel*) "Praise" (Psalms 113-118). "They mixed the **third cup** for him. He says a blessing for his food. [And at] **the fourth**, he completes the Hallel and says after it the grace of song" (m.Pesahim 10:4)

In Mark, we read this - "Truly I say to you, I will never again drink of the fruit of the vine until that day when I drink it new in the kingdom of God." After singing a hymn, they went out to the Mount of Olives. (Mark 14:25-26). The ritual seems oddly similar. The third cup, then words of thanks, then the fourth cup, followed by singing, and the meal is over. If the second-century custom mentioned in this rabbinic text was already practiced in the days of Yeshua, then his enigmatic words about one cup having a special meaning and another cup that he will not drink can be read against the set custom.

Imagine that Jesus, as the head of the banquet, just offered one of the four cups of Passover to his disciples. He tied its meaning explanation to his own blood in anticipation of what was to happen. After that, he mentioned not drinking wine until he drinks it in God's Kingdom. And then they went up the mountain singing hymns. The words they sang came from the book of

Psalms, no doubt. Such was the Passover tradition that second-century rabbinic text relates. We are even told which Psalms.

What if the Passover ritual and the words in these verses in the gospels are indeed related to the third and fourth cups the way they were described by ancient rabbis? It is very possible that Jesus turned down the fourth cup just because what he was about to experience it in a few hours aligned with the third cup? And the succession of cups has a particular symbolism in the Passover setting, which connects to his overall message for delivering Israel from slavery. The third cup had to be fulfilled, so of course, the teacher said he would not drink the fourth cup just yet. It is not time.

According to Rav Tarfon and Rav Akiva, quoted in Mishna, the third cup of the celebration was connected to God's redemption of Israel. God redeemed Israel from slavery by his own right hand (Ex 6:6). Perhaps just as second-century Jews connected this cup with the last morsel of the sacrificial lamb, so Jesus connected this third cup of Passover with his own death on Passover.

Could it be that it was the third cup of Passover that Jesus called the "cup of his blood"? We know that he charged his disciples to remember it not just as the deliverance of Exodus but as his redemption each time they drank it. This cup meant death to Jesus, but it also meant redemption for Israel. Is this the cup he visualized himself drinking? Is this the cup he prayed about that it may pass him by in the garden?

I believe that this was the cup no one else could drink from, the cup of voluntarily giving up one's life to bring redemption. That would all make sense, but only if you knew that there was a ritual involving four cups with distinct meanings attached to each cup. I do realize that these explanations take some imagination and creativity. But they are all built on historical context, on the historically-attested cultural behaviors and customs, on the order of an enduring ritual and language of that era. The language and context of Mishna and the gospels happened to coincide.

Understanding the intricacies of this colorful and rich celebration of Passover and knowing its customs helps us to understand Jesus' words in their festival context. These are very ethnically bound and cultural terms obvious to those who were there in that setting and elusive to most who have little knowledge of how Jews celebrated Passover. These folkways were no doubt familiar to Jesus' disciples since they were children, celebrating Passover from year to year. To them and the gospel writers, the cup he mentions has a specific and obvious meaning. But to most modern followers of Jesus, the words are foreign as they mention some obscure cup as an idiom, perhaps as an idiom that simply stands for his fate. See what difference insider knowledge makes?

Take it or leave it. Maybe you are skeptical of the background I supplied for you from Mishna. But whatever you think, do not stay ignorant to the deep cultural background of countless biblical passages.

Knowing the historical setting, the rituals, and customs of Israel, and when they occurred, how they took place may provide a vivid means to understand Jesus's words. The historical realities fill in the gaps that words leave unsaid.

I remember once I was on a long road trip, driving alone on the highway for miles and miles. I found an interesting radio station that aired American music from the '40s. I loved the tunes, the mastery of big band pieces, but the message of many of those catchy songs was so foreign to me. I speak English fairly well, but the songs used slang, colloquialisms, and terms I had no idea how to interpret. The performers spoke of life I had a hard time imagining because I did not know their lingo or the daily mores of the 40s. I realized I was missing something significant… Knowing the culture and what those words mean can make a difference between really understanding something or being left simply guessing. So, I loved the tunes but missed out on the message.

As I reflect on my experience of listening to the 40's music, I realize that this is how many of us experience the Bible. We appreciate it immensely, we benefit from it, but at the same time, we are puzzled by some things that make no sense to us. The picture is incomplete to us. And it's not that we are not smart or do not understand the general gist of the message. We can understand most of what we hear. We simply lack proper points of reference, so we don't get the full benefit.

I have already mentioned that knowledge of how people lived and how they understood the word is often obscured by our own culture. In Matthew's Gospel, Yeshua said to his disciple Peter, "I will give you the keys of the Kingdom of Heaven and whatever you bind on earth shall have been bound in heaven, and whatever you loose on earth shall be loosed in heaven" (Matt 16:19). A couple of chapters later he said very similar words to his other disciples (Mat 18:18).

The most common explanation about these "binding and loosing" verses that people hear today is that they have something to do with spiritual warfare and binding the devil. Indeed, the surrounding context is about the disciple's authority, only the devil is not involved here, not even remotely related to the context of these verses. Many modern Bible readers are not aware that these terms have a very specific meaning in the context of human behavior.

In the first-century Jewish context, "binding and loosing" are known technical legal expressions. The "binding and loosing" is simply older English for "tying up something" and "untying something." In Greek, "to bind" is δέω *(deo)* and the Hebrew equivalent is אָסַר *(asar)* which means "to tie up," "to bind," "to confine," "to imprison," and idiomatically "to forbid" something. (a tool I like to use to see which Hebrew terms correspond to Koine Greek is called Greek-English Lexicon of the Septuagint) In Greek, "to loose" is λύω *(luo),* and the corresponding Hebrew term is הִתִּיר *(hitir)* means "to untie," "to unbind," "to free," "to release," and idiomatically "to permit" something. So it's simple, "to bind and to loose" really means "to forbid and to permit" something.

Here is an example of these terms from the first-century Jewish writer Flavius Josephus. He explains that under queen Alexandra of Jerusalem, the Pharisees ran things.

> "...[Pharisees] became the administrators of all public affairs, empowered **to banish and readmit** whom they pleased, as well as **to loose and to bind**". (Josephus, Jewish War 1:111).

Josephus wrote that at that moment in history, the Pharisees had the authority "to loose and to bind," and no, he did not mean demons or Satan or anything of that sort. They had the legal authority to make rules and laws that governed Jewish life in Israel. Notice how Josephus uses this pair of verbs as descriptions of legislative powers. And early rabbis used equivalent terminology in their legal discussions as well.

> "…These are Torah scholars who sit in many groups and engage in Torah study. There are often debates among these groups, as some of these Sages render an object or person ritually impure, and these render it pure; **these *(bind)* prohibit** (אוסרין; o*srin*) an action, and these *(loose)* **permit it** (מתירין; *matirin*); these deem an item **invalid,** and these deem it **valid**… So too you, the student, make your ears like a funnel and acquire for yourself an understanding heart to hear both the statements of those who render objects

**ritually impure** and the statements of those who render them **pure**; the statements of those **who prohibit** (אוסרין; *osrin*) actions and the statements of those **who permit them** (מתירין; *matirin*); the statements of those who deem items **invalid** and the statements of those who deem them **valid**." (Babylonian Talmud, Chagigah 3b, Davidson Translation)

The "binding and loosing" terms may appear here in Aramaic, but the context is quite clear; it's forbidding and allowing that the rabbis are talking about. Consider another example of these same terms. There was once a contention between some rabbis from the land of Israel and rabbi Hanina. They deliberately reversed his rulings, justifying their actions that he was acting on his own and that Israel is really the final authority on matters of importance (Is. 2:3). These rulings were described as "binding" and "losing" decisions. This is what the Talmud records:

"Granted, Ḥanina would rule an item pure and the Sages from Eretz Yisrael would rule it impure; they ruled stringently. But in a case where he ruled an item impure and they ruled it pure, what are the circumstances? How could they rule pure that which he ruled impure? Was it not taught in a baraita:[5] If a Sage ruled an item impure, his colleague is not permitted to rule it pure; **if he (bound it)**

---

[5] *Baraita* is an oral teaching of the ancient rabbis which was never preserved in Mishna, and but according to memory, belongs to the generation of sages that compiled the Mishna.

**prohibited it** (אסר; *asar*), his colleague **may not (loose) permit it** (להתיר; *lehatir*)? [The Gemara[6] explains:] They held that they must do so in this case, so that people would not be drawn after him; due to the exigencies of the time they overturned his rulings."
(Babylonian Talmud, Berachot 63b, Sefaria Translation)

Clearly, the sages from Israel simply did not like Rabbi Hanina's rulings, even though he was a notable teacher. **Thus, they loosed what he bound and bound what he loosed.** So getting back to the Gospels, just like the Pharisees in Josephus's quote, the disciples were simply given a right to legislate, a right to make rules and norms, allowing and forbidding things in their own community. And that is binding and loosing in the historical context of the first century. Go ahead and reread these passages again and see if you can find anything specific in the greater context to tie those words to spiritual warfare, the devil, or exorcism. I promise you will have to imagine those settings because the literary context makes no such connections. Instead, it will become clear that in each instance, one's authority to make decisions is in focus.

I know that insisting that the Bible should be interpreted through our knowledge of history or language may not sit well with everyone. It seems so cut and dry, so scientific, so unspiritual. What about God giving us an understanding of his words supernaturally? Yes, that has

---

[6] *Gemara* is a fifth-century CE commentary on the Mishna text. Combined together, *Mishna* and *Gemara*, make up the *Talmud*.

a place, but let me explain. When I speak about studying the Bible, I mean reading the ancient words to learn something, to understand what those words were originally meant to communicate. This type of study implies seeking an objective meaning, not reading for inspiration or personal spiritual guidance.

Reading the Bible devotionally is not the same as studying. When we read for spiritual reasons, we pursue a less objective approach and very personal goals. Have you ever heard people share what some particular passage meant to them or, more precisely how it spoke to them? That is great, but that is a personal and not objective meaning. God uses such things to lead us in life, but what something means to me, because I was moved by it in a particular way, is not the same as what it means objectively.

We read the Bible devotionally because we want to hear from God. We read the Bible with a spiritual lens to gain a sense of direction for our lives. We hope that divine words will lead us to the answers we are seeking in our family relationships and at work. And often times if we are honest about our spiritual needs, if we pray and ask God for help, he leads us to the very answers we seek. But those are our answers, for us, for our headaches and problems. God will use the very same verse to speak to someone else an entirely different message. So which meaning is correct? Neither. Because we were not seeking the original historically accurate, objective meaning. We were seeking a spiritual solution to something in our lives through God's words.

We will stumble across stories of faith and examples in the Scriptures, which will encourage us and strengthen us. Sometimes what we will read will shame us and show us the error of our ways. The range of feelings and emotions our interaction with the Scriptures will produce has to do with us and where we are on our spiritual journey. This is why when we share what we gleaned from reading some passage devotionally with other people, they do not see what we see. Sometimes we are puzzled how they cannot. But it's different for them because the answers we found are just for us, for our benefit. They are on a different journey.

We call this a "subjective meaning of the text." And this is something that God's Spirit, which indwells his children, does within us. It's a bit of a mystery of how that happens exactly. We see the meaning in the Bible, but this meaning is not for the rest of the world, and we understand that it was suddenly illuminated in this way just for us. It helps us right we are, but other people will not find it just as meaningful or even helpful. When we hear from God in such a personalized way, we experience his presence. This type of Bible reading is legitimate, but this subjective meaning and not the same as the objective meaning sought in Bible study.

The focus of this short book is the study that leads us to discover the objective meaning of God's words. When we study this way, we are reading to learn and to discover a meaning that is true in general, not true to us personally. We seek to know what was said exactly and what those words meant when they were said to the audience to which they were directed. What we personally think and feel is not relevant in this initial stage of the study. We are not the authors of that meaning. For this moment, what the original audience was going through is more important than our own problems. In such a study, we realize that while Bible is for us, we were not the intended audience. When great men of God spoke or fixed those words on parchment, they had people in mind, but perhaps someone closer to them than us living thousands of years later.

Though we rightfully feel that God's words speak to us directly, those who originally transmitted those words could not have even imagined our lives. And we have a hard time imagining their lives. We seek the original meaning of words, the way in which they were meant to be understood so that we can eventually take this understanding somewhere. And once we understand that objective and concrete meaning, we may see how it can apply to us.

Having understood how those ancient words were meant, we can step back and ask the question if there are areas of our lives where these words may apply today. Maybe the ancient words don't apply to us in the same way, maybe not directly, but they still speak to us through the ages. We may not have the same problems and struggles as an original audience, but because we are humans, perhaps some parts of our lives are similar. Maybe in some ways, we find ourselves in similar situations. But this process of seeking a more personal meaning is the second step. It should occur as a reflection after studying and having understood the objective meaning of those messages.

It is good to never lose sight of both ways of reading the Bible, studying and reading for understanding is different from devotional reading. We need both. Adding a missing ingredient of history to our study is not an easy task. There are many historical books out there, and ancient sources like Philo, Josephus, or Mishna can be challenging to read. Yet sometimes, this is where the keys to understanding exist.

Every time I lecture on Revelation, I have to explain the Beast of Revelation 13 to my students. And every time, I am asked the same questions, which usually stem from a misunderstanding of how historical knowledge plays into interpreting the Book of Revelation.

> 11 Then I saw **another beast coming up out of the earth**; and he had two horns like a lamb, and he spoke as a dragon. 12 He exercises all the **authority of the first beast** in his presence. And **he makes the earth and those who live on it worship the first beast**, whose fatal wound was healed...16 And he causes all, the small and the great, the rich and the poor, and the free and the slaves, to be given a mark on their right hands or on their foreheads, 17 and he decrees that no one will be able to buy or to sell, except the one who has the mark, either **the name of the beast or the number of his name**. 18 Here is wisdom. Let him who has understanding calculate the number of the beast, for the number is that of a man; and his number is

six hundred and sixty-six. (Rev 13:11-18
NASB)

In this passage, there are two terrifying beasts. One
comes out of the earth (land), and the other from the sea.
The beast of the earth makes sure that the beast of the
sea is worshipped. The word for "beast" in plain
language is "animal" (θηρίον, *therion*), by the way. In
Genesis 1:12, when God created all life, the "land
animals" are called *theria teis geis* (θηρία τῆς γῆς), the
same word that usually gets translated as "beast" in
Revelation. And just as there are creatures of the sea and
creatures of the land in Genesis, similar categories are
used in Revelation. By using a Hebrew-English
Interlinear translation, you can quickly see that the
Hebrew of Gen 1:24 uses the noun *behemah* (בְּהֵמָה), a
common term for "cattle" and in the plural (בְּהֵמוֹת,
*behemot*) is a word for hippopotamus, in archaic English
"behemoth." So yes, we are talking about animals here.
The idea of "monsters" is often connected to the visions
of strange-looking animals in Daniel 7, which uses the
Aramaic term *cheyva* (חֵיוָה,) also a word for "animal."
But animals, even if they scare us, are not exactly
monsters.

Of course, the question that interests many Revelation
readers is the language but the identity of the beast or
animal. And in particular, people wish to know about the
"mark" (χάραγμα, *haragma*) placed on the heads and
hands. When people pose such questions about this
passage, they usually have already filled their
imagination with all sorts of interpretations about the
mark, pop culture or otherwise. So I always have to

work against already existing images and explanations, which is much harder than starting from a blank slate.

The pop culture view that this worshiped beast is the Antichrist, who will emerge before the end of the world, and his mark is required to live and do business. In the past, the mark was carving, a tattoo, a burn, but in recent years I have heard many voices of panic about credit cards and microchips as the technology of the wicked Revelation beast. Without these microchips, no one will be able to buy or sell anything. That is a genius application of first-century words to twenty-first-century technology.

Well, first of all, there is no mention of the Antichrist in Revelation. That is an interpretive import from another place in the Bible. John chooses not to use such language in Revelation. Second, the mark of the beast is not something obscure but something very concrete and specific according to the text - his name. Being informed about the Semitic concept of "name" would be very helpful here. In short, the name in Hebrew means renown, reputation, or what you are known for, not the actual name to which one answers necessarily. I have already mentioned that Jesus was called a Nazarene. But Nazarene is not his actual name. It is his reputation among the people as a prophet from Nazareth.

Revelation is such a unique book. It contains a good doze of poetic parallelism and symbolic parody. This animal (the beast) is supposed to be worshipped in a specific way. By the way, the pagan nations have been worshipping animals for ages, so there is nothing new here.[7] As a sigh of allegiance, the name of this animal was to be placed on the forehead and the on the left hand. This is a very specific practice, and here is the irony… If you are not familiar with the Jewish prayer custom of *Tefillin* (Phylacteries), you may not see the obvious parody connection.

Torah contains commandments that instruct Israelites to take God's commandments and to write them on their gates, to place them as ornaments between their eyes, to place them on their hearts (Deut 6:4-9, 11:18-21). Since antiquity, many Jews understood such words quite literally. *Tefillin* are small leather enclosures that contain rolled-up scrolls inscribed with those very commandments. Hand-inscribed scrolls with God's name and his commandments are strapped to the forehead and to the biceps of the left arm, which is pressed against one's heart during prayer. The worshipper literally wears God's name and his commandments on one's head and left arm (pressing it against the heart).[8] In the parody, the beast's name is to be a mark on the forehead and right arm. Coincidence? This method of worship expresses religious devotion and allegiance in a very tangible and visual way.

Beyond that, Revelation even tells us a couple more hints that the name of the beast can be "calculated," and it is a name of a "man" (ἄνθρωπος, *anthropos*) – a human. The name of the "beast of the sea" is six

---

[7] Iliad (8th century BCE) records the worship of animals, particularly horses. In Gilgamesh (c. 1000 BCE), we encounter the worship of the heavenly bull. In Exodus, Israelites succumb to the worship of a golden calf. Egyptians were known to worship cats, dogs, crocodiles, falcons and etc.
[8] The oldest *Tefillin* scrolls and boxes were found at Qumran, in cave 4 in the 20th century. The artifacts recovered were dated from the fifth century BCE to the first century CE.

hundred sixty-six. I realize that most Revelation readers recognize that 666 is some sort of a purposeful code. John mentions that "one who has understanding" should be able to figure it out. Though he does not say what that understanding is. This means that John's first-century audience should have the ability to know the identity of the person he lines up with the animal. The identity of the beast was known to John's readers. If you were ever frightened by Revelation 13, good news, John's explanations attach these events to the first-century CE context. And this is where the knowledge of history comes to the aid of unraveling a very convoluted passage.

Best we know, the book of Revelation was written very late in the first century CE. It originates from Asia Minor, a Roman province which in modern-day is located in Turkey. We know that Roman Emperor Domitian, who reigned from 81 to 96, was known for his persecution of Jews and Christians. The dating of Revelation is a guess since the book itself gives chronological references, but it is an educated guess that it was authored during Domitian's rule. Jews had already been expelled from Rome in 19 CE by Emperor Tiberius, and then another expulsion took place during Claudius (late forties?). That expulsion is mentioned in Acts of the Apostles 18. The exact date is uncertain, but Claudius reigned from 41-53 CE. According to historical sources, each time, the problem that prompted expulsions was Jewish success in converting notable Romans to their faith.[9] Rome was not threatened by religious pluralism, but monotheism created dissonance.

---

[9] One Roman source notes, "Since the Jews constantly made disturbances at the instigation

The writer of Revelation, John, tells us that he was in exile on the isle of Patmos. He was isolated because he was deemed socially dangerous by the authorities. Because of his position, he had to be very careful what he wrote about the state or government. It's likely that his correspondence would be monitored. Hence his language of code, which would make sense to those familiar with apocalyptic Jewish books but quite confusing to outsiders. In Jewish imagination, beasts (animals) often represent people, most often rulers, leaders, kings, and sometimes even countries. That is exactly how prophet Daniel uses strange creatures in his visions. In his visions, the animals represent kingdoms. And Revelation uses the same technique.[10]

So who is this beast of the sea or 666? The short answer is - Emperor Nero. Nero was a brutal Roman monarch known for his vicious animal-like behavior. He ruled Rome from 54 to 68 CE. So, why Nero, and not Domitian or some other wicked ruler? How can I be so certain about the identity of this beast of the sea? His name is a number that can be calculated!

In antiquity, the Hebrew alphabet functioned as both letters and numbers. If we used the same logic with English, A would be 1, B would be 2, C would be 3, and so on. Thus, any name spelled in Hebrew may have a meaning that comes from its root, but it would also have

---

of Chrestus (Christ?), he [the Emperor Claudius] expelled them from Rome"(Seutonious, Divius Claudius 25).

[10] Compare the so-called "Animal Apocalypse," one of the visions recorded in 1 Enoch with Daniel and Revelation. Many scholars believe that the vision describes the events of the Maccabean era, representing people with animals.

a numerical value. The numerical value of נרון קסר *(Neron Keasar)* "Nero Caesar" in Hebrew is 666. Coincidence?

Here is how it works (Hebrew reads from right to left) - נ (50) + ר (200) + ו (6) + ן (50) + ק (100) + ס (60) + ר (200) = 666.

So what are the odds that another combination of Hebrew letters would also add up to 666? The odds are high. The numeric value of my full name in Hebrew (פינחס שיר) is 718, for example. Minor adjustments in spelling can get me even closer to 666. The desired 666 sum can be achieved through numerous possible combinations of Hebrew letters. And it is conceivable that some of these letter combinations could be actual names or people. But John said to his audience that they should be able to calculate the name. Limiting the names to the first-century historical context, to rulers who sought divine worship from their subjects severely limits the options. What am I suggesting? It's possible that 666 could represent some other name out there, but not one that would line up with the historical setting of Revelation.

The reason why I am so confident that 666 represents Nero and not someone else is another curious historical discovery that many initially thought was a manuscript error. In one manuscript of Revelation, dated to the third century CE[11] the number of the beast appears as 616. Initially, the scholars who found the discrepancy thought it was an error made in copying. I believe it was a

---

[11] Revelation, Papyrus 115.

deliberate scribal adjustment. Irenaeus, who lived in the second century CE, mentioned 616 as the number of the beast in his book "Against Heresies," (Book 5, Ch 30, Section 1) Hippolytus, who lived in the third century CE, also referenced 616 as the number of the beast in his work "On Christ and Antichrist," (Section 36).

In Greek and Hebrew, Nero's name is spelled with N at the end (neron /νηρόν / נרון). In Latin, however, it is spelled Nero (without the N at the end). Can you guess what would happen to the end sum of 666 if the letter N is dropped and the emperor's name spelling is calculated according to its Latin spelling? It would be 616. I think the scribes who copied Revelation knew John's code behind 666. But as Latin became more prolific, the calculation of the name could fall apart. So they made an adjustment in the numerical end sum to make sure the same result would come from a different spelling.

So whether it's 666 or 616, it's still Nero Caesar. Even if some other name could be lined up to 666, applying this Hebrew vs. Latin spelling experiment, the calculations will fall apart. By the way, in the Jewish world, the meanings of names are quite significant, and νηρόν (*neron*) in Greek means "wet." I consulted Liddell and Scott's Greek-English Lexicon. So the "beast which came out of the sea" really suits his name.

If Revelation is a document written in the 90s, why is Nero, who died in 68 CE is the first beast and not Emperor Domitian? Because Nero is as bad as it gets. At some point, Nero became the quintessential symbol of pagan evil that caused havoc and travail. Just like Herod, which was a personal name but was used to represent many rulers, Nero became a name unto itself. Just as in our time, Hitler could be the name ascribed to someone because they deserve it, not because they have any relation to the twentieth-century Austrian-born leader, such is the case with Nero.

Nero is a symbol of any emperor and of everything that is wrong with Rome. Three Roman historians, Tacitus, Suetonius, and Cassius Dio, preserved details of Nero's life. In 59 CE, he killed his own mother, Agrippina, for opposing his love affair with Poppaea, who was that that time married. He eventually married Poppaea, but years later, in 65 CE, Nero kicked her to death during her second pregnancy. The same historians tell us that in 67 CE, Nero married a young boy by the name of Sporus. He had him castrated and put on a proper public wedding ceremony complete with a dowery ritual and a bridal veil. In the end, Nero's economic policies and excessive taxation caused havoc for Rome and led to elites calling for his removal. The Senate declared him a public enemy, and his life ended in suicide.

The first Jewish War against Rome started under Nero in 66 CE. Vespasian was ordered to crush the uprising. Nero died in 68 CE, but his war continued, and in 70 CE, Jerusalem Temple was destroyed. Vespasian and his son brought the destruction, but Nero called for it. Thus, it makes sense that for Israel, Nero is the supreme villain, a symbol of utter lawlessness and destruction, and thus he easily qualifies to be the first beast in Jewish minds.

Early non-Jews in Christ had to avoid imperial polytheism, which created a huge cultural divide for them. Rejecting state-mandated emperor worship put them in the category of rebels and enemies of the state. Many died refusing to give honors to people that God alone deserved. Since the days of Alexander the Great, Jews were exempt from giving obligatory honors to the gods. They paid taxes and tributes but due to their longstanding unique ethnic beliefs, were allowed not to sacrifice to deities that their ancestors did not recognize, worshipping one and only invisible God. Religion and ethnicity were inseparable in antiquity, and short of formal conversion, gentiles did not have a claim to such an exemption. If they refused to sacrifice to Nero or Domitian, they were rebelling against their own people and way of life. The book of Revelation constantly reflects these political realities. And such persecutions were real. The mark of the beast may not have been as stamp or a tattoo but it was real and without loyalty to the state people were marginalized economically.

This was a truly drawn-out explanation of the Revelation 13 passage, but adding historical background, events, people, and political shifts as an interpretive scheme takes some time and effort to explain. Much of what we know of the past are reconstructions based on multiple fragmented records. Even if you remain skeptical of my explanations about the Roman emperors and beasts in Revelation, at least I hope this explanation was entertaining.

Take it r leave it, **I remain a firm believer that history is the missing ingredient number two for many**

**people who study the Bible.** Adding it to the recipe, in my opinion, helps a lot in making sense of the Bible's message. I tried to demonstrate how I use historical knowledge step-by-step in this example above. Still, the study of history is a considerable challenge. I have already highlighted some reference materials in my examples, but naturally, that is only a drop in a proverbial bucket. There is so much more. Thus, here is my practical advice regarding the second ingredient:

[As usual, unless you seek practical advice, feel free to skip to the next chapter.]

**STEP 1:** Don't read the Bible as a modern book written in one specific era. Consider that its content spans diverse times and scenarios. Try to identify to which era the texts you study belong. Always keep the historical context of any passage at the forefront of your mind as you study. If you have ancient sources, consider the images they paint for you and the stories they tell. Look at economics, daily life, politics, and any major shifts and try to imagine what it would be like living in that era. Then try to interpret the text armed with what you know of the past.

**STEP 2:** If you want to understand the Bible objectively, avoid Bible teachers who ignore history. They offer inspiration and some food for your soul but not objective knowledge. Study with those who focus on history and affirm the Bible. Lean on those writers and commentators who know history better than you and have invested considerable time in investigating the historical background of various biblical scenarios. Be mindful of secular researchers and historians. They are usually honest and can offer excellent insights but are often biased against the Bible by virtue of their own worldview. Researchers committed to both the truth of the Bible and history are the ones most likely to help you in your pursuit of solid biblical interpretation.

::::::: I hope you are enjoying the book! If you do, would you help others discover it? It will take only 5 minutes of your time. Pull up the title of this book inside Amazon, tap "write a customer review," and leave a few positive remarks. Your feedback would be a help for me as the author and a kind service to many others considering the book. You can also drop me a quick email about your review -

petershir8@gmail.com :::::::

# THE THIRD MISSING INGREDIENT

The majority of Bible readers today know little of the culture, customs, lifeways, and social dynamics depicted on the pages of the book they love. That's all right. Most people in the world are focused on their own culture and way of life because that is what surrounds them and that is what they need to be successful in life. Studying the culture of some people far-far away, even those who lived long-long ago, a culture which is no more, seems irrelevant. Most people do not see that as something useful, and that is completely understandable.

As a result of such state of things, most modern Bible readers may have some general framework about ancient Israelite, Greek, and Roman culture in their mind, but their understanding may be too general, too incomplete, and worse, twisted and inaccurate. And that is not very helpful when it comes to studying the Bible. In fact, it can cause us to take some wrong turns in understanding the Bible.

It is indisputable that the Bible is full of rich social and cultural references tied to the time and place when those ancient words were written. Cultural references are unavoidable, and most often, they left not understood unless they are familiar. Because we are not aware of them cultural references are frequently passed by and ignored. They are often explained away in some roundabout ways. These are not malicious omissions, just our normal human limitations. We, humans are very limited in our perception of reality and rarely aware of how much we do not know.

I know that few readers of the gospels are familiar with the world of ancient rabbis such as Jesus. He was indeed addressed as Rabbi over a dozen times in three gospel records. So he was a rabbi, but what did the first-century rabbis do? I will share some background information to show how such knowledge could be extremely helpful in interpreting the gospels.

A second-century rabbinic text describes the objectives of a rabbi or a Torah teacher in the following way: The sages said **"three things: be deliberate in judgment, raise up many disciples, and make a fence around the Torah"** (Mishnah, Avot 1:1). The first two of these injunctions make sense, but what is a "fence around the Torah"?

Just like a physical fence, a fence around the Torah is a protective enclosure around a commandment; in other words, an extra layer of rules. First, one has to scale the protective fence and only then be in a position to transgress the actual holy commandment. This way, it will be more difficult for people to transgress the Torah. Sounds like rules upon rules, right? Well, for a good reason. If living righteously is the goal, then avoiding getting to close to crossing the proverbial line is a good practice. It safeguards us from coming dangerously close to sin. So fences around commandments were well-intended means of ensuring righteous living. So just like rabbis of his day, Jesus built fences around commandments too!

"You have heard that it was said, 'You shall not commit adultery'; **but I say to you that everyone who looks at a woman with lust for her has already committed adultery with her in his heart**" (Matt 5:27-28).

First, Yeshua quoted the original commandment (Exodus 20:14) and added, "But I say to you…" and then comes Jesus' fence: "avoid lustful gazing." According to Yeshua, adultery and unfaithfulness come from looking at someone or something that is not yours, and suddenly the desire is born. He says that this is already a sin. But merely looking at people is actually not prohibited in Torah. No, there is no such commandment. The fence is for protection. The goal of Jesus' fence is to avoid inappropriate gazing that leads to inappropriate desires so that one will not commit the actual sin of adultery. This is an example of Jesus building a fence around a biblical commandment, as was the practice of many other rabbis of his day.

The sermon on the mount passage is full of this technique. Unfortunately, I have seen people perform elaborate interpretive dances with these verses. If only people knew this simple technique of building fences around commandments. They could have explained Jesus' teachings so simply and cogently. Instead, each teaching of the Master built on top of the biblical commandment turns into the religious dictum vastly more spiritual and superior to the words of the Torah. Sadly, that is not what Jesus was doing in those verses. He was not giving a new or better Torah but merely reinforcing the existing one, the one he said will stand till heaven and earth pass away (Matt 5:18).

Let's face it. Other people's cultures do not always make sense to us. But then we want to take those cultural messages and have them speak to us, have them teach us something valuable, we get lost. Sorry to break it to you, but like most great stories, most wisdom books, and philosophical works, the Bible is a very culturally bound message. It cannot be homogenized to be generic and universal, to make sense to any and every human being in whatever unique worldview they possess. Most people across the world are radically different from each other when it comes to perception, language, thought patterns, values, beliefs, and life practices. And the people of the Bible, the Jews, are like that as well.

In ancient days, Israelites had a distinct agricultural practice that set them apart from the nations. They did not harvest the edges of their fields. The Torah says, "When you reap the harvest of your land, moreover, you shall not reap to the very corners of your field nor gather the gleaning of your harvest; you are to leave them for the needy and the alien. I am the LORD your God." (Lev 23:22). The idea of this agricultural charity is simple – Israelites were not to harvest everything but rather leave the edges of their fields so that members of their community in need could gather the remaining crops and feed themselves. Curiously, God did not specify how much of one's land should remain unharvested. That was left up to the individual's conscience. Israel is commanded to share their harvest blessings with both their needy brethren and foreigners living among them. The Hebrew word for the "corner" of the field in this verse is פֵּאָה (*peah*). It can mean an "edge," "border," "boundary," "side," or "corner." It can even mean "forehead" or "temple" in ancient Hebrew because they are considered the "edge of one's face." So how far Israelites were to go with such practice was a matter of the heart.

You may be familiar with the Jewish cultural practice of not shaving or cutting the פֵּאֹת (*peot*) "corners or edges of the beard." If you run across those verses, before, this might seem like a very strange commandment in the Bible. Why would God care how the Israelites styled their hair (Lev 19:27)? Apparently, our appearances matter to Almighty and they say something about us to the world as well.

Just as God expected his people to leave some produce on the corners of their fields for the poor, God also wanted Israel to be constantly reminded of this social responsibility. Their obligation to care for the neediest in their community should have been so ingrained in their lives that they would wear a reminder of this obligation on their faces. In this way, one's identity (and one's appearance) are inseparably tied to God's will for his people.

To understand the Bible, one has to be willing to enter its unique world, even in part. And that means you might have to leave your world behind when you seek understanding. Yeshua was born in Israel, a Jew, he dressed like one, ate like one, talked like one, and shared thousands of other traits and life experiences with other Jews of his day. If we are to understand his culture, we have no choice but to study ancient Judean life and its values.

One time I was asked an intriguing question, "Did Jesus use leavened bread or Matzah on Passover?" I was a bit puzzled at first. Because in my mind, of course, he used *matzah* (מַצָּה), the unleavened bread. Why wouldn't he? It's Passover, and such is the custom. So I had to clarify what exactly gave my questioner the impression that Jesus would eat anything besides *matzah* during the festival week in ancient Jerusalem. And as we discussed the topic further, it became clear that this was a really well-informed question.

I am aware that some churches use regular bread for communion: sourdough, ciabatta, baguette and etc. So my conversational partner was not alone in supposing that Yeshua actually used regular leavened bread during the "holy week." The story says:

> "While they were eating, Jesus **took some bread**, and after a blessing, He broke it and gave it to the disciples, and said, 'Take, eat; this is My body.'" (Matt 26:26 NASB)

The Gospels literally say that "Jesus broke bread" and use the Greek word ἄρτος *(artos)*. That is a direct equivalent of Hebrew לְחֶם *(lechem)*, and the word indeed just means "bread." The confusion comes from the fact that "unleavened bread" is a special term in the Greek language – ἄζυμος *(asumos)* and the passage implies he

74

used just regular bread ἄρτος *(artos)*. So the gospels do not specifically say that Messiah broke and distributed ἄζυμος *(asumos)* to his disciples on that night, so the interpretation comes straight from the original text of the Bible.

This is when it finally dawned on me that this is a simple misunderstanding based on the ambiguity of language and lack of cultural knowledge. What was a mundane and implicit fact to me was not at all obvious to my questioner.

So here is the answer I gave… Jesus did break ἄρτος *(artos)* "bread" in the gospel story, but it was during the week of Unleavened Bread (Mat 16:17). The story does not have to specify that this was "unleavened bread" because that was the only kind of bread that would have been available that entire week in Jerusalem.

Many people do not know this, but traditionally, all leaven is physically destroyed in Jewish communities one day before Passover begins. This is done on purpose, and today there is even a special ceremony. Every housewife and every baker would have made sure they had no leaven or yeast in their possession in preparation for Passover. Why? Because it is expressly commanded by God, "For seven days no leaven shall be seen with you in your entire territory" (Deut 16:4).

Yeshua's disciples would have had to make some very special arrangements to find any leavened bread around to make sure it was available to them at a time when no leaven was found anywhere in Jerusalem. And people did not bake bread to last for several days back then. It was a daily activity.

It should be noted that in Greek ἄρτος (artos) is a generic word for "bread," just like לֶחֶם (lechem) in Hebrew. In fact, ἄρτος (artos) can be used idiomatically for "food" in general. The famous prayer says, "give us this day our daily bread" (Matt 6:11). But that does not mean all we ask for as sustenance is literally bread. Some vegetables and cheese, some olives, and maybe fruit would be wonderful too. But no, the text only mentions bread. Do we truly think God gave people bread and bread alone in response to such words? Of course not. God provides all sorts of food, and that is implied and understood because bread is a synecdoche for "food" in general.

One can say that ἄρτος (artos) is a food category that can describe all sorts of bread, and ἄζυμος (asumos) or מַצָּה (matzah) as a specific variety of bread can fall under this very broad definition too. The ancient Greek translation of Exodus 23:15 (LXX) instructs to offer God ἄρτους ἀζύμους (artus asumus) "unleavened breads" to God. And even manna that fell from heaven in the wilderness was called ἄρτος (artos) "bread" in John 6:31. But was it ever even a grain product of any variety? What I am explaining is that "bread" does not have to contain "leaven" (ζυμωτός; zumotos, חָמֵץ; chametz) in order to be properly classified as "bread." This is a cultural assumption based on our modern culinary practices, based on what we think in our minds bread should be like. Few people today enjoy unleavened bread on a regular basis, but in antiquity, that was quite common.

In addition, thinking theologically, "leaven" (חָמֵץ; *chametz*) is expressly forbidden by Torah (Ex 12:15, 20) during the feast that Jesus celebrated. Eating leavened bread during the feast would turn the rabbi and his disciples into deliberate transgressors of God's laws. This is very unlikely based on Yeshua's emphasis on holiness and respect for Torah all throughout the gospels.

Thus, the kind of bread that Jesus broke and ate during his Last Supper was certainly unleavened, even if the text does not stress that variety explicitly. How do we know that for sure? In this particular case, the knowledge of Greek alone does not help to resolve the question. We can properly answer this question only by understanding the way people lived by reconstructing their life settings. There was no leaven in Jerusalem that day, so all bread was unleavened bread.

Culture is a powerful force, and it dictates how we interpret the world around us, and that includes the Bible. Fears over the recent global pandemic sent many Bible believers to seek answers in the Scriptures. While consulting biblical verses is not a bad thing, sometimes these verses are misunderstood or manipulated to suit various modern presuppositions. The use of the Bible in translation alone and ignorance of ancient culture allows people to twist the biblical text to say something they do not. I will venture to say that a vast majority of Bible readers today understand illness in a way that is absolutely foreign to how it is presented in the Bible. The culture is so different today that it reshapes what the Bible says.

Here is rarely embraced truth in the context of human health. Ancient Israelites did not have the same type of faith in medicine as most modern people do. In their worldview, sickness was not something people could manipulate, control, cure, or even prevent. It is a mistake to read the Hebrew Scriptures solely through a modern scientific lens. We must allow the original biblical language to impart meaning to us, not the other way around.

Let's consider a few biblical passages. Leviticus states, "When the infection of leprosy is on a man, then he shall be brought to the priest" (13:9 NASB). The NASB translation mentions the "infection of leprosy," but ancient people did not have designated terms for infectious disease–nor did they know about bacteria or viruses. That, of course, does not mean that the terrible effects of lingering diseases (what we call "pandemics") were absent in antiquity. But it will be hard to find the language of "infection" or "outbreak" in ancient Hebrew.

The biblical term for "infection" or "ailment" is usually נֶגַע (nega), which literally means a "strike" or "blow." In the term's verbal form, נָגַע (nega), it means "to touch." The mysterious affliction in Leviticus 13 that is most often rendered "leprosy" (צָרַעַת; tzara'at) is, in fact, a "blow" in Hebrew (נֶגַע צָרַעַת), and "infection" is a thoroughly modernized English translation.

Furthermore, translating the condition as "leprosy" makes it a common bacterial disease that can be treated with a course of antibiotics. Such translation is very misleading because, in the ancient Jewish perspective, *tzara'at* is not a pathogen with its own biological agenda but rather a condition brought on by God, fully under divine control. In other words, in the biblical worldview, God is the one who does the striking, not the disease. I realize this is a tough one for modern people to embrace.

Another English translation that may be misleading is that of "disease." For instance, Genesis 12:17 reads, "But the Lord inflicted serious diseases on Pharaoh and his household because of Abram's wife Sarai" (NIV). The "diseases" (נְגָעִים; *negaim*) in the NIV translation is the plural form of נֶגַע *(nega)*, – a "blow." The modern temptation is to associate "disease" with something contagious, like a virus, but the above verse begins, "The LORD struck" (וַיְנַגַּע יהוה). A נֶגַע *(nega)* is not a naturally-occurring contagion in the Bible but a purposeful act of God.

The use of the term "plague" in English translations makes things even worse. In light of past outbreaks in human history (such as the Bubonic plague), the word carries ominous associations for most people. The English insertion of "plague" appears in the ESV rendering of Exodus: "The Lord said to Moses, 'Yet one plague more I will bring upon Pharaoh and upon Egypt'" (Ex 11:1 ESV). Here is the surprise, the same exact noun (נֶגַע; *nega*) in this verse of ESV is translated as "plague" and not "disease or "infection." So what is it? The dance translations dance should be obvious by now. What if we simply accept this concept of sickness the way ancient Israelites did? It's a blow from God. Most modern people would associate a plague with some sort of pandemic, but that is not what the Bible communicates.

Now we have seen the same simple term translated quite differently into English from one verse in the Bible to another. I deliberately used three different popular English translations (because no translation is perfect), and they can all be misleading when it comes to matters of health and sickness. To ancient people, a "strike" or a "blow" from the LORD is not a disease, nor an infection, nor a pandemic. A biblical "strike" may make one sick, and there may be some ways to alleviate the symptoms, but God is both the source and the cure in ancient Israelite thinking. The Bible presents spiritual realities from a perspective that embraces the supernatural as a norm. So as long as we allow our modern scientific thinking to influence our interpretations, the actual meaning of biblical texts will continue to evade us.

Do you think that a rainy day is a blessing from God? Many people dislike soggy weather. Ancient Israelites believed that rain at the right time and in the right amount was an ultimate sign of divine goodness. And its absence is connected to human sin. Nonsense, right? We modern people know that weather conditions and precipitation are caused by changes in atmospheric pressure and temperature, winds and etc, not good or bad behavior. Once again, our modern scientific culture leads us away from supernatural explanations the Bible espouses.

In 1 Kings 17, Elijah announced that there will be no rain on the land because of sin. Zechariah 14:17 says that when King Messiah comes, the nations that will not go to Jerusalem every year to honor him will receive no rain. In Revelation 11: 6, the two witnesses have the power to stop rain from falling and to turn water into blood. How we live can affect the environment around us, at least the rainfall.

> Solomon prayed… "When the heavens are shut up, and there is no rain because they have sinned against You, and they pray toward this place and praise Your name, and turn from their sin when You afflict them, 36 then hear in heaven and forgive the sin of Your servants and Your people Israel; indeed, teach them the good way in which they are to walk. And provide rain on Your land, which You have given to Your people as an inheritance." (1 Kings 8:35-36)

I have mentioned Mishna before, it's a second-century CE rabbinic document, The Talmud is a commentary on Mishna from the fifth century CE. Many customs and traditions preserved in Talmud, however, come from deep antiquity. If anything, the ancient texts allow us to peek into the minds of ancient people and discover how they viewed life. From ancient texts, we see how people lived and what they considered important.

The Sages taught: "Then I will give your rains in their season" (Leviticus 26:4). This means that **the earth will be neither drunk nor thirsty; rather, a moderate amount of rain will fall.** For as long as the rains are abundant, they muddy the soil of the land, and it does not give out its produce. Alternatively, "In their season" means on Wednesday eves, i.e., Tuesday nights, and on Shabbat eves, i.e., Friday nights, because **at these times people are not out in the streets,** either due to fear of demonic forces that were thought to wander on Tuesday nights or due to the sanctity of Shabbat. As we found in the days of Shimon ben Shetaḥ that rain invariably fell for them on Wednesday eves and on Shabbat eves, until wheat grew as big as kidneys, and barley as big as olive pits, and lentils as golden dinars. And they tied up some of these crops as an example for future generations to convey to them how much damage sin causes, as it is stated: "The Lord our God, Who gives rain, the former rain and the latter rain, in its season that keeps for us the appointed weeks of the harvest. Your iniquities have turned away these things, and your sins have withheld the good from you" (Jeremiah 5:24–25). And we likewise found that **in the days of Herod that they were occupied in the building of the Temple, and rain would fall at night**. And the next day the wind would blow, the clouds would disperse, the sun would shine, and the people would go out to their work. **And rain would fall only at a time when it would not interfere with their labor,** the nation knew that the work of Heaven was being performed by their hands. (Babylonian Talmud, Ta'anit 22b-23a)

Rain was seen as a divine blessing, and the weather was shaped based on God's will and prerogative to the degree that it fell on certain times of the week but not on others to accommodate people and their needs.

So here is a custom many Bible readers do not know about. In the days of Jesus, Jews prayed for the annual rainfall in a very organized fashion. This custom still takes place at synagogues today, only in a slightly different form. It was a communal prayer for corporate welfare through ample rain, enough rain for the crops to be abundant. These special prayers are recited during the celebration of Sukkot (the feast of Tabernacles) every year. In Israel, it rains only in the winter season, so all the rainfall Israel will get will come after Sukkot and before springtime.

In Jesus's day, ancient Jerusalem was illuminated by large lamps set up in the Temple courtyard at night, and special water ceremonies took place in the Temple precincts. They are not recorded in the Bible, but Mishna tells us about them.

> They said: Anyone who has not seen the rejoicing of *beit hashshoevah* (house of the drawing) in his life has never seen rejoicing.

At the end of the **first festival day of the festival** [the priests and Levites] went down to the women's courtyard. And they made a major enactment [by putting men below and women above]. And there were golden lampstands there, with four gold bowls on their tops and four ladders for each landholder. And four young priests with jars of oil containing a hundred and twenty logs, [would climb up the ladders and] pour [the oil] into each bowl. Out of the worn-out undergarments and girdles of the priests they made wicks, and with them they lit the candlesticks. **And there was not a courtyard in Jerusalem which was not lit up from the light of *beit hashshoevah*.** The pious men and wonder workers would dance before them with flaming torches in their hand, and they would sing before them songs and praises. And the Levites beyond counting played on harps, lyres, cymbals, trumpets, and [other] musical instruments,[standing, as they played] on the fifteen steps which go down from the Israelites' court to the women's court corresponding to the fifteen Songs of Ascents which are in the Book of Psalms— on these the Levites stand with their instruments and sing their song. And two priests stood at the upper gate which goes down from the Israelites' court to the women's court, with two trumpets in their hands. [When] the cock crowed, they sounded a sustained, a quavering, and a sustained note on the shofar. (Mishah 5:1-4, Neusner Translation, modified)

The customs described in this texts are beautiful and deeply spiritual. I believe that a considerable section of the Gospel of John is set to these very events. And by knowing the customs and prayers people prayed during ancient Sukkot celebrations, Jesus' teachings in John ring a very unique way.

John 7:1 and 10, say that Jesus was present at the Feast of Tabernacles (Sukkot). During the water libation ritual in John 7:37, he called out to those who are thirsty to come to him and drink. He promised to give them living water. These are all well-known verses that gospel readers sought to understand for ages. Only most Bible readers do not know that these words were uttered at the very moment when the priests would sing songs about living waters from the Psalms and Prophets. Yeshua said what he said because it fits the context of the celebration, in reflection of the ceremonies that took place in ancient Jerusalem (Mishna, Sukkah 4, Babylonian Talmud, Sukkah 48b-49a). Study the first-century Sukkot customs, and all of a sudden, Jesus' words make sense.

In John 8:12, Yeshua called attention to himself as the "light of the world" and said that if people follow him, they will not walk in darkness. What does not mean? Because of the late-night ceremonies at the Sukkot festival, many worshippers walked through the dark streets of Jerusalem at that very moment. There were no streetlights back then. There was no nightlife in first-century Jerusalem. The sun went down, and generally, people stayed home, ate meals, and went to sleep. But during this festival, some people carried torches, and thousands of visitors streamed towards the mountain top, the temple, which was artificially lit up for the festival (Babylonian Talmud, Sukkah 5a). Once the first-century customs of Sukkot are properly surveyed, many of Messiah's teaching come into sharp focus. His words had a direct bearing on what was going on all around him.

It is important to know our limitations when it comes to reading ancient texts. There is nothing wrong with realizing that we lack the proper context, proper knowledge, and data and do not have good points of reference. It is liberating to be honest about this, even when we read the Bible. God's message is powerful, and most of the time, even if we do not fully understand every little detail, we will still benefit from it. God will use the smallest tidbits we understand to do his work deep within us. That is the mystery of faith and walking with God. Thus, as you may have guessed, **Awareness of culture and customs is the missing ingredient number three.**

I will be honest, offering practical advice to advance in this area is not easy. Mainly because culture and customs are all around us. And studying such a broad and expansive area of human experience is not as easy as picking up a couple of books.

[Feel free to skip ahead, unless practical advice is what you seek.]

**STEP 1:** Be mindful of the culture in the Bible. When you encounter a behavior that seems odd or out of the norm, consider if this is a special custom of the people at that time. When you come across statements or actions that seem abnormal, consider that this is a particular cultural way. In Exodus, Israelites needed to collect some gold, so Aaron told them to take the gold rings from the ears of their daughters, wives, and sons (Ex 32:2-3). Strange fundraising strategy. But apparently, in that generation, Israelites all wore earrings. Abraham asked his servant to swear an oath by holding on to his private parts. (Gen 24:2). An odd way of seeking assurance. Today we would ask people to sign an affidavit. But it worked for them. There are many things that will not make sense to you because they are customs and cultural expressions. Seek to understand their meaning first and foremost. Consider what a particular custom communicates and what values or sentiments it expresses.

**STEP 2:** Commit to becoming more culturally aware when it comes to the ways of the East. Any list of books that inform us about culture would be vast and incomplete because culture is so expansive. So I would suggest starting with general and encyclopedic resources. I have already mentioned Cultural Backgrounds Study Bible. That is a good place to become aware of the role of ancient culture in biblical contexts. But there are more specialized books out there, like the Oxford Handbook of Apocalyptic Literature, if you are studying apocalyptic ideas. Or if you want to understand Jewish life around the first century, there is

*The Oxford Handbook of Jewish Daily Life in Roman Palestine*. There are just so many great reference books out there. Books, especially books, in particular, can get pricy. Unless you have access to a good library, a solution that I personally have made great use of is digital books available through Logos Software packages.

# ADDING THE MISSING INGREDIENTS

There are more missing ingredients out there, but I will stop at these three because I believe they are central and pivotal: Language, History, and Cultural Context. I am convinced that these three ingredients are missing in many people's Bible study today, and in fact, they have been missing for thousands of years. As soon as Jewish followers of Jesus, who lived very similar lives to many biblical characters have faded into the fog of history, many cultural and linguistic connections were lost to non-Jewish followers of Christ. It's a sad reality, but Jews who believed in Jesus were marginalized to the degree they simply disappeared in Christ-following communities. Such is often the fate of minorities. Those who continued to live a Jewish life and follow their ancestral ways were criticized so harshly for being different inside the church for centuries. Until there was no one left. So finally, there was no one to provide this context anymore.

Most church fathers were trained in Greek philosophy and oratory but not the Jewish Bible or its interpretation. Great matters of theology were debated by people who only read the Bible in Greek translation and may not have even had access to the whole Bible as we know it. Over the centuries, many brand new ideas were added to the biblical texts, and many novel explanations arose over time in biblical interpretation. Why? Because the interpretations of the Bible did not lean on ancient knowledge anymore, but only recent knowledge. A method called *sensus plenior*, for example, caused absolute havoc for biblical interpretation. There is nothing wrong with *sensus plenior* if it is understood as only one of the methods of understanding the biblical text and not the solely preferred method.[12]

But Israelite culture has such a long history of biblical interpretation. Hillel was a renowned Jewish sage who lived during the first century BCE. He's well-known for his teachings on morality and ethics and his many contributions to Jewish law. One of his significant contributions was the "Seven Rules of Hillel," which are principles of interpretation that help scholars understand the meaning of the Hebrew Bible.

The Seven Rules of Hillel were developed to address the complexities of the biblical text and are influential in Jewish biblical interpretation even today. The rules are: (1) *kal va-chomer* (from light to heavy), (2) *gezerah shavah* (equivalence of expressions), (3) *binyan av* (analogy), (4) *hekkesh* (comparison), (5) *tofel ve-yored* (part and whole), (6) *kelal u-prat* (general and specific), and (7) *prat u-kelal* (specific and general). Hillel's Seven Rules of Interpretation provide safety guidelines for interpreting the Hebrew Bible and doing so consistently. These rules help apply logic and reason to the interpretation of biblical texts, allowing for a better understanding of textual nuances.

---

[12] Writers such as Origen and Augustine have leaned heavily on *sensus plenior* interpretations (Latin for "fuller sense"), a method articulated by the 17th century by the Dutch theologian Johannes Cocceius.

The rabbis of 12th and 13th centuries recognized four basic levels of interpretations of any basic passage that always coexisted and called them using PaRDeS as an acronym.[13] *Peshat* is focused on literal historical and grammatical interpretation. *Remez* considers hints the passage contains to related ideas, expanding the meaning of the passage. *Drash* is focused on theological exposition aimed at moral conclusions and practical life applications of biblical teaching, often looking way beyond the immediate context. And *Sood* zeroes in on a symbolic, esoteric level, often hidden and encoded ideas meant to be discovered by those who seek them.

Jews have been studying the Scriptures as a community for many generations, passing on traditions and commentary from father to son, and teacher to student. So many volumes have been written to explore the meaning of God's words over the ages. Sadly, because most Christians think that Christianity is not Jewish and has nothing to do with Jews, they have no idea such knowledge even exists r can be relevant to them. Very few venture to find out what is out there.

When Christians lost their connection to Jews, they robbed themselves of immense spiritual wealth. This is another one of those missing ingredients, but I purposefully decided not to address this one in the book. The mistrust between Jews and Christians is a longstanding and complicated issue. I would only say that when students of the Bible discover what it is like to

---

[13] As a method, PaRDeS is utilized in "Sefer HaPardes" by Rabbi Jehudah HaLevi (12th century), "Sefer HaBahir" by Rabbi Nehunia ben HaKaneh (12th century), "The Zohar" by Rabbi Moses de Leon (13th century) as well as works of Ibn Ezra (12th century).

study with those who continue to live many of the things most Christians only read about, it transforms their perspective. It's a tragedy that I wish to see remedied.

I hope you do not feel discouraged or frustrated at the moment that some key ingredients are indeed missing in your Bible study recipe. Now that I have shown you how the biblical text can unfold by using these ingredients, your desire to add these components to your study would be only natural. That is why I do not want to end my discussion of these missing ingredients on such a low note. I believe I can not only make you aware of what is missing, but I can help you start incorporating some of these missing ingredients on whatever level you are ready for.

When you know that something is missing, don't go on as if nothing is wrong. Change it! We live in an amazing era. Like no other time, we can access so much data, so much information, and often completely free. The key is to know what you are looking for so you can seek answers it in the right places. You probably do not have the time or stamina to sit down and learn a couple of ancient languages. Ancient history may be fascinating, but you don't even know where to begin reading thousands of pages of ancient lore. It's a maze, I know. I understand all the usual excuses. I have heard them many times, and some of them I have voiced myself for years.

The cultural study is perceived as something a bit more accessible. You may have some Jewish colleagues or friends, well-educated friends, in fact. So you can ask them all sorts of questions about their culture. But let's face it, they do not think like Moses, feel like King David, or complain like Jeremiah. They cannot even imagine the lives of Luke, Cornelius, or Matthew. Their modern Jewish experience is hardly comparable to the culture of Jesus or the apostles…I hope you see my point. Competence in modern culture gets us only so far.

So what is the solution? I am going to disappoint you for just a moment by being blunt. There is no hack, easy fix, or shortcut. I suggest you surround yourself with people who know the very things you are missing. Prolonged exposure to these things will lead to a degree of competence. If you are serious about the kind of Bible study I have been describing, find a place where you can explore biblical languages and study the historical background and ancient Jewish culture. See what my weekly e-zine www.pshir.com has to offer.

Peers and community is a big plus. Make some new friends and acquaintances, if you must, to achieve your desire. Study with them and learn from them when you can. Join a study community of others like yourself who seek to recover what is missing, and you will be surprised how helpful your peers can be to you! Begin to delve into these areas, and you will grow and understand more and more each day. In the era of instant gratification, I am suggesting that it will take time to achieve this aspiration. Sorry to disappoint, but that's the reality.

If you embark on this path, with time, you will connect the dots in entirely new ways, and you will see the results of how your perception of the Bible was suddenly altered. The journey will enhance your Bible reading and will open new avenues of understanding for you. It may be a bit scary, but that is because all new things are at first scary to us. Sometimes we must step out on faith. Keep the living faith you have at the heart of your study, and do not allow the pursuit of information and knowledge to lead you away from living your faith.

Whatever you do, just don't go on knowing that something important is missing and do absolutely nothing about it. At the very least, join some educational YouTube channels, subscribe to some blogs or podcasts that have the mission to bring out the original language meanings, engage by reading relevant history, and consider pertinent cultural contexts in explaining the Bible. Maybe take a suitable course or two to remedy what is missing in your Bible study.

I am a big proponent of distance learning, lifetime learning, and digital education. Join me and my colleagues if you would like at Israel Bible Center if you can. Just do something about it that works in your particular circumstances.

# HARMFUL INGREDIENTS

This is a chapter I had to write. Initially, I hoped to avoid it, but then as I sat down put my thoughts into writing, I realized that I had no choice. If I want to present a balanced view of how the Bible can be studied better, I must mention a least a few "harmful ingredients" that can ruin one's Bible study recipe as well. Unfortunately, these harmful ingredients are many, and they are common. But since this book is not really about harmful ingredients in your Bible study, I will try to be quick about them as I offer some words of caution about them. I will focus only on three: Personal Cultural Bias, Anachronistic Thinking, and Turning General into Absolutes. Don't get angry with me if you suddenly realize you are currently utilizing these harmful ingredients. I am just the messenger.

## Personal Cultural Bias

We all have biases, several of them at a time usually. I know I do, and I can probably list many of my biases and presuppositions in my thinking. I am not one hundred percent objective, and I know it. There are many things I take for granted. These are my axioms, my most basic foundations, and presuppositions. For example, my core bias is that "God is." Anything that I think about is built on this basic presupposition. I never think about anything as if God is not in the equation somehow. I suppose I could, but that would be difficult and unnatural for me. Another presupposition or bias that is a part of my worldview is that God opted to work through Israel as his chosen people in this world. And that is something that is unchangeable until all history as we know it culminates. These ideas are two examples of my basic assumptions which I always carry with me. I can go on, but I think my point is made. Your assumptions and biases may be different from mine, but you certainly have them. Our biases shape the very framework through which we analyze everything around us.

All of us by virtue of being human and finite in our knowledge struggle to understand the world around us. We do the best we can. And as we figure things out, we make assumptions, estimations, and judgments. Often, we do not have the full picture, so we can be completely wrong and not even suspect it. If you don't think you can be wrong about things in life, if you are one of those people who is always right, please stop reading right now and close this chapter. Find something else to do, because I am only going to annoy and upset you in the paragraphs to follow.

A bias is a condition we all have to live with. It's like a chronic illness in some way, an ailment that will never go away completely. It is not bad or evil, it is quite normal and natural. The harmful side of things is when we are blind to the fact that we have a particular bias. The danger is when we have no humility and we think that we are one hundred percent fair and objective. Even if we are honest, we can never fully escape our bias and subjectivity, but we can be aware of it and keep it in check. We can put it aside from time to time to see something well outside of our usual box. This is what many scientists try to do as they seek to discover something new.

We are all culturally conditioned, and since our culture constantly paints an image for us of what this world is all about, it becomes innate to see the world through the eyes of our own culture, whatever it may be. And that works well until we encounter something outside of our culture, something which is contrary and makes no sense, something in conflict with the reality we know and understand. That is when things do not line up, and we experience tension in our understanding. Either we let go of our presuppositions and our bias and allow ourselves to reconsider something that makes no sense without them. Or we hold on to the bias and reject that which is in tension with it. Alternatively, we can minimize the problem we face by explaining away the tension, so it does not pose a challenge to us anymore. This is how we function unconsciously when our usual thinking is challenged.

Why am I explaining all this? Because unless you are an ancient Israelite, a middle eastern Semite, living an agrarian or pastoral life, much of the Hebrew Bible and New Testament will challenge your thinking. The world of the Bible is foreign to most of us. We must recognize that we read the Bible through our own cultural lens, whatever it may be. I can illustrate this through our occupational proficiencies. I imagine that a judge or a lawyer keeps seeing loopholes and legal issues in the Bible. I would suppose that many medical professionals are tempted to diagnose the exact conditions of those who were brought to Jesus for healing or exorcisms. And I would suspect that an accountant or an economist would be drawn to the analysis of Bible passages that describe economic transactions, commerce, and monetary systems. Each reader of the Bible brings their own unique context and their own world with them as they seek something for themselves in those ancient words. And when we seek something, we often find that very thing we seek. Allow me to illustrate this with a short story.

Have you ever wished you did not hear or see something? What we see and hear is hard to put back into a box of non-existence. Once we experience something, we simply cannot put it out of our minds. Basically, we can't unknow what we know. This is true when it comes to interpreting the Scriptures. Knowing the context of any passage usually helps immensely in interpretation. The original languages help too, but sometimes what holds us inches away from a better interpretation is what we know, or rather, what we have been told. It's the truth we embrace. Take this verse from the Gospel of John.

> "If you forgive the sins of any, their sins have been forgiven them; if you retain the sins of any, they have been retained." (John 20:23 NASB)

A seemingly simple verse, very straightforward teaching. It is very easy for Catholics to interpret but a tough one for non-Catholics. Is Yeshua really saying that his disciples have the power to dispense the forgiveness of sins? It sure looks that way. They can also choose not to issue forgiveness, and those sins will remain. The Protestants naturally struggle with sin absolution as they recall the practice of church selling indulgences in the Middle Ages, one of the reasons why Protestants came to be. And for Jews, this teaching makes no sense either. This stubborn verse is hard to ignore and explain away. How else can one read it except that the apostles have the power to dispense forgiveness of sins to anyone they deem worthy?

One way the Protestant tradition deals with this verse is to suggest that this is not about "forgiveness" but about the proclamation of salvation. In other words, the word "forgive" is not to be understood literally. If they proclaim the available forgiveness of sins to people, the people will have their sins forgiven, but if they withhold the message, those people will not receive the forgiveness (because they will not know about God's gift of grace). Such a twist essentially makes this verse about evangelism. I do not know if this explanation satisfies you. Me… not so much.

By the way, I am not putting down Catholics or Protestants for their respective beliefs, but let's look deeper into the context. There is another way to see this teaching. First of all, there is a key phrase many people miss that precedes this passage. Verse 21 says, "Peace be with you; as the Father has sent Me, I also send you." This means that this greater story is about Messiah sending his messengers out into the world to continue his mission. And the rest of what he says could be related to this sending. He breathes on them, giving them the spirit, and then talks about forgiving people's sins. This is the surrounding context of the saying in question.

Secondly, there is another important tidbit of information. The verb ἀφίημι (*afiemi*) is typically translated as "forgive" and κρατέω (*krateo*) as "retain" as in "not forgive." But there are also alternative ways to translate these key verbs in this enigmatic statement. For example, ἀφίημι (*afiemi*) can also mean "let go," "release," "leave," and even "allow." And κρατέω (*krateo*) "hold on strongly," or "hold back, "restrain," "grasp," and even "rule." Allowing these alternative translation choices, we may see some alternatives and can read this verse in a new way.

Thirdly, this verse sounds so much like Matthew's binding and loosing promises. "I will give you the keys of the kingdom of heaven, and whatever you bind on earth shall have been bound in heaven, and whatever you loose on earth shall have been loosed in heaven." (Matt 16:19)

> "Truly I say to you, whatever you bind on earth shall have been bound in heaven; and whatever you loose on earth shall have been loosed in heaven. "Again I say to you, that if two of you agree on earth about anything that they may ask, it shall be done for them by My Father who is in heaven. For where two or three have gathered together in My name, I am there in their midst." (Matt 18:18-20 NASB)

It is also interesting that just after this explanation of the legislative power Yeshua gives to his followers, Peter asks a question about, you guessed it... forgiveness. "Then Peter came and said to Him, "Lord, how often shall my brother sin against me, and I forgive him?..." (Matt 18:18-19). This brings me to a very simple point. Who says that "If you forgive the sins of any, their sins have been forgiven them" (John 20:23 NASB) is about forgiving the sins which were committed against God? There is absolutely nothing in this text to suggest that the disciples are dispensing forgiveness for the sins which constitute transgressions against God and his laws.

My simple assertion is that this text is about letting go of the offenses that were committed against them, against the disciples! After all, Yeshua is sending them out into the world. Their message will be rejected (just as he was rejected). "As my Father sent me, I am sending you." Yes, some people will mistreat them. They can choose to let that go, and those sins will not be held against those individuals who mistreated them. But if they choose to hold on to those offenses, those who mistreated them will have to answer for their actions later.

In Jewish tradition, people are encouraged to seek forgiveness directly from those whom we have wronged. Jews do not ask God to forgive them for mistreating a fellow human. When it comes to sins against God, people are to take those matters to God. When transgressions are against people, the customary admonition is to settle those matters directly with them. The wronged party holds power to personally forgive and let go of those offenses against them. This is a fundamental Jewish value of *teshuvah* (repentance).

The interpretation I offer is a very simple alternative, a very straightforward interpretation. The only part that changes in this verse is what type of sin the disciples are forgiving. Each one of us has the power of not holding on to the pain caused to us, and forgiving the offenses other people perpetrate against us. The teacher says, "if you forgive those sins, they will be forgiven to those who harmed you." This power of personal absolution is always within our grasp. But to forgive the sins that others sinned against the Almighty himself... well, that is a tough one. And clearly, I do not see this passage actually teaching such practice.

If we have such broad authority, would there even be a judgment at the end of times? That is not the end that I remember reading about in the Bible. Hopefully, now you see what I meant by saying that sometimes a simple interpretation is just inches away. But the things we have been told before, the ideas we hold too firmly in our minds, can hold us back from seeing it clearly.

Many people have gone through the Bible for centuries and tried to westernize it, anglicize it, to create cultural bridges with their own cultures to understand it better. It's admirable. So many attempts have been made to straighten out its message so that it does not clash with the worldview of its readers. That is problematic because now we could be changing what God actually said. Bias and conditioning we being to all things in life is a powerful force, especially if we do not recognize that it is guiding us. We if are blind to our bias, it will mislead us.

Is there a cure? I propose a simple ABC strategy to deal with bias and to minimize it. First, *admit* to yourself that you do not know everything, and as a result, you have holes in your understanding. You may have made wrong conclusions about theology, Bible, and even people's lives. Admit such a possibility to yourself on an ongoing basis. Never stop thinking that you have arrived to a hundred percent of anything, and you will be on the way to minimizing your personal bias.

Second, *balance* yourself by committing to listen to well-reasoned and logical opinions and perspectives you may even disagree with. You should be able to at least hear out some educated perspectives which you yourself do not embrace. Don't dismiss them before hearing them out. Work to understand the arguments of those with whom you disagree. You may still think they are wrong after all is said and done, but the process is the goal. A wise person should be able to entertain an idea as a hypothesis without fully embracing it just to see if it will work or not. There is nothing wrong with an experiment or a test. When tests fail, we rule out those things we tested and move in. Practice this approach from time to time to balance your bias, and you will keep it in check.

Third, *commit* to embracing some new ideas. If you do not know everything, then it is possible to learn new things which are also true. Never stop expanding your understanding of the world, and never stop rethinking the information and ideas you already know. Add to knowledge. Do not close off your mind to new discoveries, new evidence, or new analysis of old evidence. Commit not to stagnate intellectually or spiritually, and this open-minded approach will help you with your bias blindness.

As humans, we are creatures of our environment. We are profoundly influenced by our cultural environment and social circumstances. This influence drives our perception of everything that surrounds us, and you guessed it, that includes the Scriptures. You will never get rid of your bias entirely. But at least you will know how to recognize it by admitting it, balancing and committing to modifying it through growth.

**Anachronistic Thinking**

What is anachronistic? Basically, it's judging things outside of their proper time. This is when we project our recent knowledge, recent understandings, and contemporary ways into the past. And then interpret the information from antiquity as if this contemporary knowledge was already a part of the equation and available to everyone back then. Anachronistic thinking is applying what you know today and ignoring that such thinking did not exist in the past. The Bible comes from the past, and we have to remind ourselves of how that changes things we know and embrace.

It is very difficult for us to unknow what we know, to forget the things we know. What we know today affects how we see the past, and that is a hard factor to escape. It is a struggle. We project our modern knowledge, our enlightened and progressive ideas into antiquity, forgetting that such ways of understanding simply did not yet exist. Ancient people did not know about stars and planets, and galaxies as we know them. They may have believed that the land was flat or that there was an edge to it. They did not understand meteorology and precipitation. Microorganisms, bacteria, and viruses were unknown to them. Electricity was foreign to them when they saw the lightning flash across the sky.

And here is a big one... Most people whose words we read in the Bible today have never read the Bible themselves. They did not have the Bible lying on their lap as they wrote. They could not quote and cite other texts unless they knew and memorized them. Maybe they had access to a scroll, but even that was not common. Some scrolls were available to them but only to a few, and certainly not the whole collection as we have today. Our thinking, our knowledge our system of preserving knowledge is fundamental to us. We cannot live without it and struggle to imagine how anyone else would do that.

Allow me to share an example of anachronistic thinking I see almost every day. One of my deep academic interests are texts that describe food and eating. Since the Bible comes from Jewish culture, most people know that Jews have some peculiar eating habits and taboos. The Bible clearly teaches about them, and most people today, very educated people who write on biblical topics call them kosher laws. But you see, the idea of kosher and unkosher is not biblical.

Leviticus 11 and Deuteronomy 14 articulate what should be eaten and what should not be eaten by Israelites without ambiguity. However, the terminology of Kosher vs. Unkosher is indeed not biblical. It does not appear in the Bible. Torah uses the terms טָהוֹר *(tahor)* "clean," and טָמֵא *(tameh)* "unclean." By bringing non-biblical terminology into our modern conversations about ancient Jewish texts concerning food, we bring a lot of confusion.

> "make a distinction between the unclean and
> the clean, and between the edible creature
> and the creature which is not to be eaten"
> (Lev 11:47).

Let me put it this way. Moses had no idea what Kosher is, because that concept and terminology did not yet exist in his day. It appeared much later in history. Applying such terms anachronistically to Leviticus, we imbue the ancient texts with meanings they could not have had.

How would you feel if someone wrote in a biblical commentary that Moses took out his iPhone and sent Aaron an SMS? You would not accept that a serious commentary or an accurate portrayal of biblical events, would you? But biblical commentaries use the term Kosher to explain the specifics of ancient biblical texts all the time, and no one feels that anything is out of place. I have a hunch that the majority of people simply do not know what Kosher actually means and where this term comes from.

The word *Kosher* comes from Hebrew כָּשֵׁר *(kasher),* which means "fit" or "proper". This term derives not from the Bible but from post-biblical rabbinic theology. Conversely, non-kosher food is called *Treif* comes from Hebrew טְרֵפָה *(terefah),* which means "torn," describing an animal not slaughtered but rather attached by a predator (Ex 22:30). While the Torah describes animals as either clean or unclean, over millennia Jewish tradition developed an idea of "fitness of food" called כַּשְׁרוּת *(kashrut).* And while the laws of *Kashrut* are concerned with whether the animal fits into the clean or unclean category, that is not what determines whether the animal is Kosher.

In other words, based on the Jewish law developed by the rabbis centuries after the Bible was completed, a biblically clean animal can still be considered non-Kosher. And the reason is simple. *Kashrut* is a legal category that relates primarily to the "method of slaughter" שְׁחִיטָה *(shechitah),* not the origin of the meat. The clean status of an animal is an assumed prerequisite in the Jewish food context. A perfectly clean animal slaughtered improperly is actually *non-kosher* according to the established tradition.

Today, for the meat to be designated as *Kosher*, a proper slaughter is done with חַלָּף *(chalaf),* a very specific type of knife. Proper slaughter is concerned with the absence of blood in the meat (Gen 9:4, Lev 17:10–14, Deut 12:23–24) because it is expressly forbidden. But another major concern of modern *Kosher* slaughter is the minimized suffering of the animal. The animal must be killed by a single cut across the throat. The cut must be of precise depth, in a specific area, quickly and simultaneously severing arteries, veins, nerves, trachea, and the esophagus. The animal dies instantly without suffering as all blood leaves the body naturally. These are the primary requirements that determine whether the meat would be *Kosher* or not. You will not find this in Leviticus.

You may even be familiar with the term *Glatt Kosher*. This is yet another level of כַּשְׁרוּת *(kashrut)* that emerged more recently in Jewish life. It has to do with the internal organs of the animal. In order for the meat to be labeled *Glatt Kosher,* the internal organs must be inspected and deemed to be healthy. But the *Kosher* concerns do not stop there. In recent years the Conservative Synagogues instituted a special certification called *Magen Tzedek* (shield of justice) to reflect the ethical aspects of *Kashrut* and *Eco-Kashrut* concerns, down to the details of how the animals are raised (free-range vs. confined) and what they are fed.

Think to yourself right now and consider how far these ideas are from biblical ideas and concerns about consuming proper food. And you are right. We never stand still. Biblical notions are very different and concerned with much simpler matters. The issues we face today with chemicals and commercialized food production are not in the Bible. Modern *Kashrut* concept now expands to non-meat products as well, to dairy, vegetables, toothpaste, detergents even bottled water. As a category, *Kashrut* is complicated and is well beyond the instructions about cleft hooves in the Torah. Perhaps now it is clear that when someone says something is *Kosher,* this is not the language of the Bible. We are using modern Jewish terms framed by modern food concerns and try to connect them to biblical texts anachronistically.

The Bible speaks of proper slaughter and the absence of blood in the meat, which is of clean origin and thus acceptable for consumption. The modern idea of כַּשְׁרוּת *(kashrut)* takes it to a whole different level, adding a long list of post-biblical innovations and requirements that did not exist in antiquity. So did Moses prescribe Israelites to eat *Kosher*? Or did he say simply not to eat the meat of animals which are unclean, meat that contains blood, animals that died of natural causes, or were torn up by the predators? Perhaps through the quick overview of the modern *Kashrut* criteria, the difference between the terms "clean" and "kosher" is now more obvious.

Hopefully, I did not lose you with my extended discussions about food. I am fond of the topic and have studied it from so many vectors over the years. Here is another example of anachronistic thinking that affects our interpretations. It is very common to think of Paul as a Christian. After all, so much of what is called Christian is based on his teachings which are a part of the Scriptures all Christians recognize. But surprisingly, Paul did not actually refer to himself as a Christian. That is a misnomer. Defending himself before procurator Felix, Paul said the following:

"I admit to you, that **according to the Way** which they call a sect I do serve the God of our fathers, **believing everything that is in accordance with the Torah** and that is written in the Prophets" (Acts 24:14 NASB).

"The Way" was the name of the movement that the Jewish Apostle mentioned. Standing before another council, Paul identified himself as "a Pharisee, son of Pharisees." Surprisingly in this passage, he does not say he was a Christian who once used to be a Pharisee (Acts 23:6). Paul implied that he was still a Pharisee.

Defending himself before King Agrippa, Paul insisted that he always "lived as a Pharisee according to the strictest sect" (Acts 26:5). Once again, Paul says he was a Pharisee! Was he trying to mislead the king? Did he lie to the council in Acts 23:6? The Apostle spoke these words long after his encounter with the risen Christ on the road to Damascus. Someone may argue that Paul lied, and others will insist that he told the truth. But one thing is clear, Paul does not call himself a Christian in the New Testament.

Of course, Paul was a follower of Christ. There is no dispute about that. But for some stubborn reason, he constantly chose to identify himself over and over with his Jewish heritage, calling himself a Pharisee or a follower of the Way but not Christian. There were groups of Jews in various cities across the Mediterranean who followed Jesus, but they also never thought of themselves as a separate religion and identified themselves only as "The Way."

In fact, it is also common to hear that before Paul became a follower of Christ, he persecuted Christians. You can probably guess what I am going to say next. Acts 9:1-2 text says he persecuted not Christians but "the Way." These were Jews who believed that Jesus was the Messiah. And non-Jews have not joined that movement until much later. This happened with greater frequency after Paul's revelation of Jesus.

"Now Saul, still breathing threats and murder against the disciples of the Lord, went to the high priest, and asked for letters from him to the synagogues at Damascus, so that **if he found any belonging to the Way**, both men and women, he might **bring them bound to Jerusalem**." (Acts 9:1-2 NASB)

Does it make a difference whether we call it "Christianity" or "the Way"? To a serious student of the Bible, it does because the Bible says what it says for a reason. And historical accuracy is very important when speaking of antiquity and reading the Scriptures. Even in the city of Ephesus, Paul proclaimed the teachings of "the Way" in the Synagogue (Acts 19:9), and the disturbance that occurred there had to do with the teachings of "the Way," not Christianity. Paul preached the gospel (the good news) of Messiah, but he never preached "Christianity."

Sorry if I am shocking you with this. It is not my aim to upset people by stressing this point over and over. But you are welcome to re-read all the biblical citations I provide. No mentions of Christianity (in the original texts). I know this is how people describe and interpret these events, but that is not how the texts speak of them.

If this all sounds strange, its because we are used to seeing the world from our contemporary point of view. For many people today, the gospel and Christianity is something that is one and the same. That is how they encounter these ideas in their lives. In fact, it's hard to imagine one without the other, I bet. Everyone knows that pickles go with olives, bread goes with butter, and cheese is paired up with crackers. This is intuitive, but only in some cultures and only today, and not three hundred years ago. There I digressed to food examples again. Let's get back to historical accuracy and accepting what the text says and does not say.

To a historian, Church, and Christianity are post-gospel developments. There was no Church in the gospels. There was no Christianity as an organized religious institution when Paul was alive. And by the way, the same can be said of Judaism. Judaism as an organized religion also did not yet exist at that juncture. There was no unified system called Judaism just yet. In fact, Ἰουδαϊσμός *(iudaismos)* mentioned in Gal 1:4 should probably be translated as "Jewish way of life," not Judaism, to be fair to history. In the first century, there was Paganism and also Hellenism – the Greek way of life and the universal practice of recognizing many divinities. Of course, the opposite of Paganism, there was a Jewish way of life and Israelite culture. But Judaism – Ἰουδαϊσμός *(iudaismos)* in the first century should be understood as ethnic, familial, religious, and cultural way, an affiliation which demanded loyalty to one God of Israel and was expressed in a specific lifestyle of Judeans. It is tied to Jerusalem and usually to the Temple as the central institution, not a religion.

What about Christians? Yes, that term already existed in the first century. In Acts 26:28, King Agrippa accused Paul of wanting to make him into a Christian. The author of Acts 11:25 tells us that many non-Jews embraced the good news as Jews from Cyrene proclaimed salvation in Antioch. And these non-Jews were indeed called "Christians." Peter also uses this term in his sobering teaching:

> "…to the degree that you share the sufferings of Christ, keep on rejoicing, so that also at the revelation of His glory you may rejoice with exultation. If you are reviled for the name of Christ, you are blessed, because the Spirit of glory and of God rests on you. Make sure that none of you suffers as a murderer, or thief, or evildoer, or a troublesome meddler; but **if anyone suffers as a Christian**, he is not to be ashamed, but is to glorify God in this name." (1 Peter 4:13-16)

In its earliest form, the term Χριστιανός *(christianos)* "Christian" or a Christ-follower, was a very politically loaded term, affirming one's loyalty to the Jewish Christ, in opposition to Caesar and the gods of Rome.

Judeans had loyalty to their ancestral God, and that loyalty was understood in national terms. Thus Χριστιανός *(christianos)* "Christian" was not merely spiritual but a political identity also closely tied to Israel and Israel's God. After all, Christ means Messiah (מָשִׁיחַ, *mashiach*), and that term has no meaning in Greek outside of the Hebrew Bible and Jewish prophetic hope.

Most Christians today do not see this term through such a national or political lens because they don't live in a world governed by people who equate themselves with Roman deities. Our current environment alters this perception. No doubt, as people spread the good news of Messiah's sacrifice beyond the Jewish circles and more non-Jews embraced this teaching, the term came into more frequent and broader use. Eventually, the situation and perception has changed, and the meaning changed, giving birth to a modern connotation. Now Christianity is well-known and common, but very few people have even heard of "The Way."

So, was Paul a Christian? Maybe in some roundabout way, but certainly not in his own words. As a Jew, Paul's loyalties to God and Israel were clear. He did not need another name to express his belonging to Christ since Messiah is a Jewish hope. Perhaps, being a Jew and a Pharisee who followed the Messiah was enough for Paul. But calling him a Christian who preached Christianity would be us, modern people projecting something which had not yet taken place in history, an anachronism.

The tendency to apply later ideas and force them into texts where they do not exist can change those texts and lead us away from their proper understanding. This is not a good ingredient for any recipe and a bad habit that needs to be broken. Thus, I deem this practice a harmful ingredient. These kinds of ingredients move us further and further from the truth.

## Turning General into Absolute

Translations from one language to another can be misleading, and sometimes important ideas and concepts do get lost in translation. As diligently as translators work, the readers still wield their own power to misconstrue the meaning of the text. The context becomes extremely valuable in such cases. All too often, general language references very common to English can become the enemies of sound biblical interpretations. Simple words like any, all, every, everything, none, no one, always, never, and etc. are very problematic in the Bible. We use such words rhetorically in speech, as exaggerations, as generalizations, and most often not in a literal way. General words like these, when taken at their face value, as absolutes, when reading the text narrowly, literally, excluding sensible possibilities, can make the Bible sound absolutely nonsensical. Intrigued?

On a road trip with my family, I make a stop. I walk into a gas station with my wife and say to her, "I am so thirsty!". My wife asks, "What do you want to drink, Dear?" I say, "Anything! Please, get me something good", I say as I head for the restroom. I get back to the car, and she hands me a quart of engine oil. "You said 'anything'…" – she smiles at me. Well, I did say "anything," but what I meant was "anything within the scope of normal things I would typically drink." In my general speech, I implied water, juice, soda, lemonade, iced tea, or something of that sort. So, yes, a quart of Pennzoil, a bottle of Windex, and even some Tabasco sauce are certainly all liquids. Hypothetically they are all drinkable, but that is not what I meant by "anything." My "anything" was limited in scope, and I did not articulate that scope. It was implied in my remark that "I was thirsty."

Just as it is in life, in the biblical text, there are natural contextual limits to interpreting general references like these. By the way, this is a made-up story. And it was meant to be comical and ridiculous. But that is exactly what people do with biblical texts and general references. They apply them way too broadly! The moral of this story is that we should not build our narrow interpretations and especially theology, on verses with general references such as "any," "all," "everything," "never," "always," etc., taking them in the most literal and broadest way possible, applying them in a universal and comprehensive manner. When we do this, we are prone to misinterpret and violate the natural and contextual scope of their meaning.

Now think for a moment how many Bible verses do you know that contain general references similar to the ones I already mentioned? I am going to have some fun with Apostle Paul's wirings for a moment. Warning! I will abuse these verses for the purpose of illustrating an idea…

> "for **all have sinned** and fall short of the glory of God" (Rom 3:23)

All have sinned… Wait a minute… has God sinned? Does this include Jesus? Holy Spirit? Angels? Well, it says "all," and all means all, correct? Wait… the context. Maybe all does not mean "absolutely all," and perhaps not every time and in every instance? I think maybe it means "all people," but why does it say "all"? Confusing…

> "For even when we were with you, we used to give you this order: if **anyone is not willing to work**, then he is not to eat, either." (2 Thess 3:10)

I see this is simple… Grandpa does not go to work anymore. He says he is old and tired. He worked enough in his life and wants to take it easy now. He is definitely not willing to work, so based on this teaching, he should not eat! God's word says it – I believe it. Hmm, and just to think, all this time, I have been feeding my kids for nothing. They do not really work! They really are not willing to work. I cannot even make them pick up their toys, which is not even a real job. Well, it says here, "anyone not willing to work," and that has to be inclusive of all people. Does this apply to Grandpa and kids too? Unless "anyone" does not mean "absolutely anyone," but some specific people who are a part of this

specific context and this particular discussion. Hmm…
It's not that simple.

> "For **everything created by God is good**,
> and **nothing is to be rejected** if it is received
> with gratitude" (1 Tim 4:4)

God created all things well. Interesting… There are
some things I have been wondering about for a while
now. Maybe I should try them? I am not so sure they are
good for me, though. Well, Paul says as long as I receive
them with gratitude, as long as I am thankful to God
who made them, I can go for it. Wow, that's everything
God created! That's really broad. I love Paul, he just
made it simple and allowed me pretty much everything!
The verse does say "everything,"… but I wonder if
"everything" really means "absolutely everything" or
only "some things" within the category of things he
talking about? I take it back, I am not so in love with
Paul. He confuses me.

I am being ridiculous on purpose. Sorry if I pushed my
illustrations too far for your taste with these examples.
But you saw my warning. You can probably think of a
number of similar verses with general references on
your own. I hope you see the interpretive problem we
can create when we push common general references
like everything, all, no one, always, never, a bit too far.
You may have even memorized some Bible passages
with these general references. So here is a test.

Think of a Bible verse you know well with any of the
general referees I mentioned or one you can think of.

Can you explain the natural context, the topic, and the scope of the discussion within each of the verses that you know by heart? Can you remember what the surrounding context is about? Can you remember the main points of the chapter or section where these verses are located? Are you sure you understand those words in their natural and organic context? You know the verse, but do you know how it fits into the bigger picture?

These examples from apostle Paul remind me of a comical conversation I once had with a pastor. I was speaking in his church, and as was his custom, as a polite host, the pastor wanted to take me to lunch. So he asked me if I ate kosher. So I told him, "I do." His reply to my answer was, "Boy, I am so glad Paul wrote Corinthians, and I do not have to worry about that!" At first, I smiled politely, but then I could not hold back my response. In his own jovial way, he was sort of making light of my practice and, at the same time, theologically justifying his own dietary practice. So I retorted, "Pastor, the barbeque is out, but if you buy me a nice salad for lunch, I will be glad to share why the Corinthians does not help me or you here at all." Needless to say, this turned into a fun lunchtime conversation between two people who care a lot about what the Bible says. If you are curious, this is the verse this pastor had in mind.

> 25 **Eat anything** that is sold in the meat market without asking questions for conscience' sake; 26 for the earth is the Lord's, and all it contains. (1 Cor 10: 25-26)

As we sat down to eat, I pulled out my phone and read the verses from Paul out loud to refresh our memory. So I said, "pastor, Paul says, eat what is set before you, no questions asked!" and he nodded. In fact, I continued, "he said, 'eat anything.'" Here is one of those general words that people can choose to understand in the broadest sense possible. After all, anything is anything! Did he really mean anything? And here it is, the apostle of Jesus Christ, in his own words, says that anything can be eaten. The pastor was wondering where I was going to go with that one but had a sense I may end up with a very different direction from his own.

It always surprises me how many interpreters see this statement as some sort of apostolic waiver to literally eat just about anything in sight. It is not. So I noted, "meal ingredients is not what concerned the apostle in Corinth. Contrary to the popular notion, Paul is not hinting at Jewish food laws in this passage either (Lev 11. Dt 14). In fact, Paul was not addressing Jews who discriminated between "clean" and "unclean" in his letter to Corinthians. They are not the audience here. And there is no reason to think that Corinthian Christ-followers were guided by the Israelite food laws. That would be most unusual. Instead, Paul's teaching focuses on the sinfulness of idolatry. In 1 Cor 10:7, 14, Paul says, "Do not be idolaters… my beloved, flee from idolatry". Christ-followers, Jews and non-Jews alike were absolutely barred from knowingly eating food offered to pagan gods."[14] In the following verses, Paul puts limits on his "eat anything" policy.

---

[14] Consider some of these passages to add to my point: Dt 4:15, Lev 19:26, Is 42:8, Acts 15:20; 17:29

27 If one of the unbelievers invites you and you want to go, eat anything that is set before you **without asking questions for conscience' sake**. 28 But if anyone says to you, "This is meat sacrificed to idols," do not eat it. (1 Cor 10: 27-28)

When a choice before you undermines your faith and commitment to one true God – abstain, don't do it! When your food choice communicates to an idolater that idols are just fine, don't do it. It may be legally permissible, food is food, but it would be a bad witness to your faith (1 Cor 10:23). When one becomes aware that a choice before them is clearly unacceptable before God, it is no longer a choice. Ignoring this would show disloyalty and signal that one is willing to dismiss God's ways. Such a problem arises frequently when one has chosen a path radically different from one's upbringing or a path foreign to the majority. Being in the world and not of the world is hard (Rom 12:2).

Perhaps for Corinthians, this idea of thoughtful restraint was a new idea, but freedom has its limits. God freed Israel from slavery to Pharaoh, but as they came out of Egypt, he gave Israel many specific commandments in the wilderness, and among them were commandments about what animal species they may and may not eat (Lev 11. Dt 14). God limited Israel's dietary freedom in some aspects. And these limitations pointed back to God's own holy nature. So I continued, "pastor, this teaching in Corinthians about eating anything is clearly not about kosher and non-kosher food. It is about idol-tainted food, which both you and I, as believers in one true living God, are barred from. This is what I meant when I said this verse does not help me or you."

As you can imagine, the conversation did not end there, but I will spare you the rest of it because most of it is not relevant to the limits of making general terms like "anything" into absolutes. Hopefully, my example from a real-life discussion made the point.

I did set my host's mind at ease, though, as I explained, "As far as barbeque goes, don't worry, pork is not evil, and shellfish is not sinful either. It's just to my people God repeatedly said they are forbidden "to you" (לָהֶם, *lahem*).[15] The fact that God opened the doors of his salvation to the nations does not suddenly eliminate the Torah's dietary restrictions for Israel. God put limits on our dietary freedom for a reason. We may know why, but he knows best. You are not allowed to eat idol-tainted food, but for me, the limitations go beyond that."

Our lunch turned into a very interesting conversation about all sorts of things, far beyond kosher food but mostly grounded in the Bible. But I tell this story not to explain my perspective on dietary restrictions. I wanted to show how context helps us to understand God's words immensely. Pushing general words beyond their naturally intended limits to an absolute meaning will usually violate the intended meaning of the biblical text. Taking general statements like "eat anything" by understanding that they should not be taken as absolutes

---

[15] For details see Lev 11:4-8, 10, 12, 20, 23, 26-29, 31.

is a sensible practice in biblical interpretation. Paul did not mean absolutely anything by "anything."

General terms are very common in English, and there is nothing wrong with them. But we desperately need the context to understand the way they are being used properly. We need the context in order not to twist, stretch, or exaggerate their meaning! Words matter, but the context changes everything...

::::::: I hope you enjoyed this book! If you did, would you pull up its title inside Amazon, tap "write a customer review," and leave a few thought and reflections? You can also drop me a quick email about your review - petershir8@gmail.com Your feedback would be appreciated by me personally and many curious readers on Amazon :::::::

# IN CLOSING

In a well-known sci-fi movie "The Matrix," the lead
character Morpheus tells a young programmer Neo who
wants to understand how the world around him really
works, how it is all an illusion, a computer program.
Neo does not understand, so Morpheus tells him that it's
hard to explain. It is something that needs to be shown.
He offers Neo a choice "Take the blue pill, wake up, and
forget we have met. Take the red pill and see how deep
the rabbit hole goes". The "rabbit hole" is a reference to
Lewis Carrol's story "Alice in Wonderland." In Carrol's
tale, Alice discovers a strange and bizarre world when
she follows the rabbit deep into his whole.

Sometimes when I invite people to examine a biblical
text deeper and in its linguistic, cultural, and historical
context, I feel a little like Morpheus. Especially if the
discussion is centered around a well-known Bible verse
that people think they actually understand very well. I
show people something that is right in front of them, but
they have never seen it because they have been looking
at it from a completely different vector. Sometimes I
feel a little guilty because I ruin the bliss of organized
simplicity by introducing variables that can change
everything. People are happy thinking that they have
things figured out, sorted out, and categorized. And I
come along and tell them that the words they have been
so focused on are not even in the bible verse they love
so much. The original texts says something very

different from the way their favorite translation renders it. I feel uneasy sometimes running it for people.

They never saw what was right in front of them because they had settled on what this text meant a while ago. They have accepted a particular interpretation without truly examining it. No, no one duped them. They just never looked deep and never asked the right questions. I come along and ask those questions. And suddenly, they have no answers or the answers they have, fall short of being convincing.

It is natural to accept the familiar, well-known, or common opinion and the majority view people hear espoused over and over. We are human, and we are busy living our lives the best we know how. Our perception is limited, and we only focus on the things that concern us at that moment. The human brain is amazingly efficient. It quickly rationalizes the world around us and files the data into neat, organized categories for later reference. If we stopped to think critically about everything, we would stand still, paralyzed, staring into space. Our minds take cognitive shortcuts because they must.

So sometimes when I take familiar Bible verses and offer a completely different take on them, I feel like I am disrupting something, ruining something people are quite happy with. But then, as Morpheus said to Neo, "All I offer is the truth, nothing more, nothing less," Neo decided to go for it, and I hope you as well understand the value of pursuing truth and my intentions. My goal in describing and illustrating the missing ingredients is to empower people to set aside any illusions and go after the truth. I mentioned in my introduction that my book was not written for someone new to the Bible. I want to help those who want to see more, who, after years of study, know that something is missing. It's for those who are ready for what is next.

I am a firm believer in developing an attitude of exploring the Bible deeply and allowing the texts to speak for themselves even when their message clashes with our understanding of reality. This is not an easy or quick task. And that means breaking out of the established categories from time to time. We created those categories and definitions in a rush when we first encountered something that required explanation. But maybe today, it's time to move beyond.

I hope that you had a glimpse of how deep the proverbial rabbit hole can go. Maybe you began to see how much more can be discovered by using the missing ingredients I showed you. And I hope you are brave enough to add these missing ingredients of language, history, and culture to your biblical study. If you are, go ahead and experiment with your old Bible study recipe and see what comes of it. Maybe someday I will hear about it.

Made in the USA
Monee, IL
10 August 2023

40806087R00080